John Nevin

College chapel sermons

John Nevin

College chapel sermons

ISBN/EAN: 9783337266189

Printed in Europe, USA, Canada, Australia, Japan

Cover: Foto ©Lupo / pixelio.de

More available books at **www.hansebooks.com**

COLLEGE CHAPEL SERMONS

BY THE LATE

JOHN WILLIAMSON NEVIN, D.D., LL.D.

PRESIDENT OF FRANKLIN AND MARSHALL COLLEGE, LANCASTER, PA., AND FORMERLY
PRESIDENT OF THE THEOLOGICAL SEMINARY OF "THE REFORMED CHURCH
IN THE UNITED STATES" AT MERCERSBURG, PA.

EDITED BY

HENRY M. KIEFFER, D.D.,

OF THE CLASS OF 1870,

AND COMPILED FROM THE EDITOR'S NOTES OF THESE SERMONS
TAKEN AT THE TIME OF THEIR DELIVERY.

WITH AN INTRODUCTION

By W. M. REILY, Ph.D.,

PRESIDENT OF THE ALLENTOWN FEMALE COLLEGE.

———•———

PHILADELPHIA:
REFORMED CHURCH PUBLICATION HOUSE,
907 Arch Street.
1891.

TO

THE MEMORY OF

JOHN WILLIAMSON NEVIN, D. D., LL. D.

THIS VOLUME

Is Inscribed.

A STUDENT'S GRATEFUL TRIBUTE TO THE NAME OF

A VENERATED TEACHER,

AND AN AFFECTIONATE ACKNOWLEDGEMENT

OF THE BLESSINGS OF

HIS MOST VALUED INSTRUCTIONS

AND

MOST CHRISTIAN EXAMPLE.

THE EDITOR'S PREFACE.

It is a subject of very frequent remark, and of very general regret, that the late Dr. John Williamson Nevin left so little of his profound teachings in permanent form. Though a man of the greatest ability, and most eminent amongst the leaders of thought in this country, he bequeathed very little to posterity upon the printed page, "carrying with him when he died," as Dr. Thomas G. Apple, one of his fellow-professors, has well expressed it, "the greatest and best part of all his powerful thoughts."

True, we have his "Biblical Antiquities," written at Princeton: and his masterly articles in the old *Mercersburg Review* remain to us, a most rich treasure of theological and philosophical thought; while many pamphlets, addresses and newspaper articles still continue to exhibit, to those who may be so fortunate as to have the opportunity of reading them, the masterly grasp of his wonderful mind. But beyond this, very little remains to us in printed and permanent form.

Especially is this true of the remarkable sermons delivered by him to his students at Mercersburg and Lancaster, concerning which it is well said in "The Life of Dr. Nevin," by Dr. Theodore Appel—"His great sermons, very many of them, were well worthy of preservation in book form, although he never thought of anything of the kind. Now they live only in the memories of those who heard them. At the present day they would be quite as valuable to thoughtful readers as his published articles or books. In the latter he addressed the head; in the former he appealed much more to the heart."

With the exception of an occasional discourse prepared for a special purpose, it was never the custom of this great man to write out any of his sermons. From the beginning to the end of his ministry his sermons were prepared without writing, inasmuch as, very early in his pulpit work, he discovered that in the preparation of a written sermon he invariably fell into "the essay style," which he conceived to lack, in his own case, the freedom and force so highly desirable in the preaching of God's Word. The practice of preaching without the written manuscript, adopted thus early in his ministry, gained for him the high commendation of his revered father, who conceived it to be every way more agreeable to the custom of the Church than the lately introduced novelty of sermon reading; and the method adopted in his early days clung to him to the end of his life. As a consequence of this, his life-long custom, there remain no manuscripts of any of those most truly thoughtful discourses which he delivered, on ordinary occasions, to his intelligent congregations at Mercersburg and Lancaster, composed, for the most part, of his students, his fellow-professors and their families.

With the purpose of rescuing from oblivion at least the substance of a few of these remarkable sermons, this volume appears. A few words may be needful to explain the method and manner in which the sermons herein contained have been preserved.

It was the custom of the editor of this volume during his undergraduate days at Franklin and Marshall College, at Lancaster, Pa., and during his course in the Theological Seminary at the same place, to take very full and careful notes of many of the sermons delivered by Dr. Nevin in the College chapel. This he did simply for his own personal benefit, and with no special purpose, at the time, of turning his manuscripts to any account subsequently. Being accustomed to taking down Dr. Nevin's lectures, on the week-day in the class-room, on the Philosophy of History, Æsthetics and Ethics, which, like his sermons, were always delivered extemporaneously from a few scant notes (and with such inspiring freshness and power as those who were privileged to hear them will never forget), the editor of this volume had acquired some facility, perhaps, for his self-imposed Sunday task. The notes, being rapidly taken in pencil, were fully written out shortly after the delivery of the sermon, and while it was still fresh in mind, and then laid away with no thought whatever of the use they were to be put to twenty years afterward.

And well do we remember how the venerable Doctor used sometimes to look sharply down at us from the pulpit on the Sunday, as we were busy with paper and pencil, no doubt wondering what we were at. We were afraid that he might, perhaps, be somewhat annoyed by our actions, though we were bent upon no mischief certainly. He never called us to account, however, but let us alone in our quiet corner with our work, whatever it might be.

Well, also, do we remember the outward, and in some regards the untoward, circumstances in which these sermons were preached. The chapel in our days at college was rather a cold, bare and uninviting-looking room. There rises before the mind, as we think of it, the plain, gray, rough-cast walls; the long, narrow windows of clear glass (afterwards frosted, indeed, but not much improved by the process), without ornament or decoration other than shades of uncertain material, and age equally uncertain; old-fashioned settees, painted yellow; a cabinet organ in the choir-loft; a small, white-painted altar in front of the pulpit, the pulpit itself being also white in color and elevated on a platform, which struck the beholder as being perhaps a trifle higher than either good taste or convenience would suggest—art had certainly bestowed but a modicum of its riches on the old College chapel. The very chair occupied by the preacher was of the most ordinary kind, without upholstering or ornamentation, until the year 1870, when a change was observed. A note appended to the MS. copy of a sermon preached by Dr. Nevin, and given in this volume, on "The Way of the Transgressor," says: "This sermon was preached on a very stormy day, March 27th, 1870; on which day, be it known unto you, that three certain antique walnut pulpit chairs, of a Gothic style, made their first appearance in the College chapel, being the gift, we are told, of Mrs. —— Ellmaker." This was the first sign of any attempt at the improvement of the appointments of the chapel. In the year 1873, however, the College chapel was enlarged and improved; but at the time of which we speak, it was plain and bare even to the verge of Puritanic simplicity.

But, Dr. Nevin was there; and they who were amongst the favored few in being privileged to sit beneath the sound of his voice, might well be oblivious to the extremely plain and bare surroundings—might well excuse the absence of the charms and graces of ecclesiastical art, mural decorations,

> "And storied windows richly dight,
> Casting a dim, religious light—"

in consideration of the presence of a man so truly great. Very strange it seems, too, that a man of such masterly ability should have preached on the profoundest themes to congregations so disproportionately small; for at no time during our college days did the venerable Doctor address more than about two hundred souls on the Lord's Day, the students always constituting the bulk of the audience. He should have had thousands to hear him!

But Dr. Nevin was not a popular preacher. The ordinary hearer could not well understand him, his thoughts being usually too profound, and his language probably somewhat too scholastic. It is commonly admitted that, in the ordinary sense of the word, he was no orator. Yet there were times, and these neither few nor far between, as every old student of his can well recall, when without having recourse to any of the rhetorical accessories, but relying purely upon the power and greatness of his thought, he spoke as men are seldom heard to speak—times when pouring forth truths well-nigh too great for utterance, he held his auditors spell-bound, himself at such times being quite as deeply and powerfully affected as any amongst his hearers. His manner was always somewhat hesitating, especially in the commencement of his address—a peculiarity due, it is thought, to his early determination to preach extemporaneously—and sometimes he paused painfully for a word; but as he warmed up in the discussion of his theme, this hesitancy gradually ceased, and the full tide of his thought began to come rolling in grandly upon the hearer, with magnificent sweep and overwhelming power.

It argued no small degree of general intelligence in the hearer that he could understand and appreciate the discourses of this remarkable man. For this reason it was, no doubt, that many persons in ordinary assemblies found difficulty in listening to him. They could not keep pace with his thought. Well does the writer recall the bewilderment with which he first listened to this truly great man when he went to college in the fall of the year 1866. Dr. Nevin was at that time engaged in preaching a series of sermons on the Prologue to the Gospel of St. John. These discourses were rather in the nature of exegetical comment than ordinary sermons, being very profound and masterly expositions of this most profound part of God's word. And well do we recall how utterly incomprehensible they seemed to the writer, then a Freshman at college. How much would we not now give for some such poor report of those remarkable lectures as we have been able to make of other sermons of Dr. Nevin's taken (and understood—let us be thankful for that!) at a later day.

Nor is it at all to be wondered at, as something unaccountable or even strange, that Dr. Nevin was not commonly understood or even appreciated by ordinary hearers. Like all great leaders of thought, and founders of schools, he necessarily addressed the few rather than the many. Nevertheless he did reach the people eventually—not directly, but indirectly, through the many students whom he trained in philosophy and theology. The Reformed Church in the United States has been very largely moulded by his thinking, and to him many a preacher within its communion owes a debt he never can repay; while more than a few of his students, now in positions of influence in civil life, some of them in lofty station, are applying to the affairs of state the philosophical principles wherein they were trained by him when they were boys at college.

With delightful recollection, and with feelings akin to reverence do we recall that venerable man of God, as we knew him in our College days, in the class-room, and in the pulpit of the College chapel on the Lord's Day; a man of grave and venerable appearance, and most impressive presence; his pure white hair a crown of glory, and in his face the outshining of a great mind and a noble soul. Though seemingly stern and severe, yet was there never a more truly kindhearted man, nor a teacher who enjoyed in a higher degree at once the respect and the affection of his scholars. The very presence of such a man in an institution of learning must always be of vast account, quite aside from the actual amount of information imparted in the class-room. Such a man carries an atmosphere with him—the moulding and powerful atmosphere of a strong and noble personality. And it was truly something very beautiful to see how, without exception, the students of Dr. Nevin looked up to him, admired and loved him.

The Sermons herewith given to the public are not, by any means, what Dr. Nevin himself would have made them, had he written them out with his own hand. In order that those readers who are not familiar with his style may have some opportunity of seeing what kind of work came from Dr. Nevin's pen when he wrote out a sermon with his own hand, it has been thought well to append one such discourse to this collection. No little difficulty has been experienced in making a choice; but it has seemed well to present that here given, a sermon entitled "Nature and Grace," being "A Baccalaureate Sermon preached to the late graduating class of Franklin and Marshall College, on the evening of the last Sunday in June, 1872, in the First Reformed Church of Lancaster, Penna.," and afterward published in *The Mercersburg Review* for October, 1872—a most able and most admirable discourse, truly!

The rest of the sermons, taken from our own note-book, do not profess to be exact and verbal reports and reproductions, such as an accomplished stenographer might furnish. They are merely notes taken by a student during his under-graduate days at college, and subsequently during his course in the Theological Seminary; but, having been taken on the spot, it is believed that they will be found to reproduce, with some degree of fidelity, the peculiar style of Dr. Nevin, both as to the thought and the expression. As the rays of the sun's light in passing through some unworthy medium necessarily lose somewhat of their original brilliancy and power, even so has it undoubtedly chanced in this case. Still, it is hoped that these utterances of a great mind, though given to the public in this poor way, may be found to retain at least something of those remarkable qualities which they possessed for the fortunate hearers at the time they were spoken.

The words of Arrian in his dedicatory letter, prefixed to his edition of *The Dissertations* of his venerated preceptor, Epictetus, come to our mind as being in a measure appropriate to this publication—"I did not write the words of Epictetus in a manner in which a man might write such things. Neither have I put them forth among men, since, as I say, I did not even write them. But whatever I heard him speak, those things I endeavored to set down in his very words, so to preserve to myself for future times a memorial of his thought and unstudied speech. Naturally, therefore, they are such things as one man might say to another on the occasion of the moment, not such as he would put together with the idea of finding readers long afterwards. . . . To me it is no great matter if I shall appear unequal to composing such a work, and to Epictetus none at all if any one shall despise his discourse; for when he spoke, it was evident that he had but one aim—to stir the minds of his hearers towards the best things. And if, indeed, the words here written shall do the same, then they will do, I think, that which the words of sages ought to do. But if not, yet let those who read them know this, that when he himself spoke them, it was impossible for the hearer to avoid feeling whatever Epictetus desired he should feel. But if his words, when they are merely words, have not this effect, perhaps it is that I am in fault; perhaps it could not have been otherwise."

It will be found that these discourses contain some valuable comment on the Church Year. The Church Year possessed great significance for Dr. Nevin, although he always exercised a wise freedom in the observance of it, following the spirit rather than adhering to the letter. This is evident from the fact that his texts were always chosen in harmony with the leading theme for the "Lessons of the Day," but were never slavishly confined thereto. This habit is well illustrated in the sermon on "The Law of Spiritual Vision," in that on "The Glorious Prince of Salvation," and in others contained in this volume.

The date given at the end of each sermon marks the time of delivery.

The Editor herewith gratefully acknowledges his obligations to the following persons:

To Miss Alice Nevin, of Lancaster, Penna., and to her brother, Wilberforce Nevin, Esq., of New York City, for permission to use the plate of the portrait of their father as a frontispiece to this volume.

To the Rev. Dr. D. M. Wolf, of Spring Mills, Penna., for valuable assistance in the notes of one of the sermons herein contained.

And, finally, to the Rev. Dr. Wm. M. Reily, President of the Allentown Female College, for his most generous assistance and his unfailing encouragement during the preparation of this work, with the sincere belief that but for him it would never have been undertaken or brought to completion.

May these discourses, presented in this way to the Church, be blessed of God and accomplish great good in the present generation, as they so eminently did when spoken from the pulpit of the College chapel to a generation of professors and students soon to pass from the scene of earthly trial, labor and care.

H. M. KIEFFER.

THIRD ST. REFORMED CHURCH PARSONAGE,
Easton, Pa., June 1, 1891.

INTRODUCTORY NOTE.

BY REV. W. M. REILY, PH D.

The aim of the editor of this collection of sermons in giving them to the public is, and of course should be, none other than that which their author had in view in preaching them. It is certain that the latter would have said that it is all contained in the familiar words of our Lord: "And this is life eternal, that they might know thee, the only true God, and Jesus Christ whom thou hast sent." John 17: 3.*

* The following is from a sermon on " Give us this day our daily bread," preached before the Synod which met at Easton, October, 1878: "'Thou hast given him power over all flesh, that he should give eternal life to as many as thou hast given him; and this is life eternal, that they might know thee, the only true God, and Jesus Christ whom thou hast sent.' What does such language mean, if not that the whole Gospel is comprehended in the manifestation of God, brought to pass in the accomplished glorification of Christ's humanity as it could be in no other way? This was the supreme object of his incarnation. 'To this end was I born,' he says, 'and for this cause came I into the world, that I might *bear witness to the truth*.' Whatever may be said of other doctrines then, they can have no real worth or force except by comprehension in what he himself makes to be the sum of all when he says, 'Father, glorify thy Son, that thy Son also may glorify thee.' This is the doctrine of all doctrines; the article, we may truly say, of a standing or falling church. But how little, alas, we hear of it in our evangelical pulpits and schools at this time! Our

Of pious and most worthy parentage, and reared under the influence of a high order of Christian culture, Dr. Nevin early consecrated himself to the gospel ministry. His ideal was a lofty one, and nothing was left undone to render himself "a workman that need not be ashamed, rightly dividing the word of truth." * Accompanied by the blessing and prayers of a God-fearing father, he went through a full collegiate course, and then entered the Theological Seminary at Princeton. Here he so far distinguished himself for prudence, industry and talent, as well as Christian earnestness, that he was chosen to the temporary position of an assistant professorship in that venerable institution of learning. As a monument of his scholarship at this early age, we have the well-known work on "Biblical Antiquities," which the American Sunday-school Union engaged him to write.

Surely he must be regarded at this time as fully equipped for the great work of life which he had in view, that, namely, of preaching the blessed Gospel of the Son of God. "Yes," some one may say, "theoretically at least." But read the "Antiquities," and see the spirit of the man! Everything bears evidence of a life in closest contact, not only with the written word of Revelation, but with that divine and eternal

---

Christianity is weak for want of it; and can have no strength against the "armies of the aliens" (infidel science and Roman superstition), so long as this want endures. That is the *revival* the church now needs; and it can come only from the Lord, as a new epiphany through his Word; as the prophet of old prays: 'Oh, that thou wouldest rend the heavens, that thou wouldest come down, that the mountains might flow down at thy presence, as when the melting fire burneth;—to make thy name known to thine adversaries, that the nations may tremble at thy presence!'"

*Chrysostom explains the Greek word translated "rightly dividing" thus: "We praise even those husbandmen who cut their furrows straight; so also the teacher is to be commended, who follows the canon or rule of the Divine Oracle." A modern commentator adds, and describes the method of Dr. Nevin well in the words: "One who wanders not to the right or the left, but goes forward directly in the path of truth who, at every step, takes for his rule the revealed Word of God."

order of being whence it springs, and of which it is the bearer and representation.

If there was one idea stamped upon the mind and memory of Dr. Nevin by his profound and extensive studies in the Old Testament, it was that of the Hebrew prophet. In the history of the pre-Christian world are nowhere to be found characters so deserving as these of the predicates "great and strong." He here learned what it is to be a prophet of God. Jehovah chose only those to be such who had a deep sense of the force of past revelations, who knew the meaning as well as the history of God's covenant with Israel, who were ready, at any cost, whether of health, comfort, name, life itself, jealously to vindicate the conditions of that covenant, both in the form of defending and comforting the faithful, and rebuking and condemning those who violated it. Such men as these were not only called by God, but endowed by heavenly inspiration, and supported by heavenly agencies. He found thus that what he had consecrated himself to was not the phantasm of a vain imagination, as, alas, is so often the case, but an office whose outlines were clearly defined before his mind, an office which, on the one hand, involved self-sacrifice, courage, fidelity, patience, but, on the other, was attended by unspeakably blessed promises.

Just as these Israelitic heroes bore witness for the truth, in the name and instead of Jehovah, so would this young preacher devote himself to the work of witnessing for Christ,—this work—nothing more, nothing less.* But in one respect,

---

* The following is from manuscript notes of a sermon on "Christ, the King of the Truth." "When we receive the truth, then do we emerge from the dark and narrow prison cell of the natural understanding, and receive a knowledge which comes from above, and Christ Himself will put His seal to it that the truth which we receive comes from God. He is 'the first-born of every creature,' and being in Him we shall know the truth, and shall bear witness also, in our own lives and persons, to that truth. Oh, how solemn the Christian ministry, under this view, as being in its very nature a personal witness-bearing to Him who is the Truth, as well as

beside, of course, many others, he differed much from them. They were men that lived among the people, and understood the people. And when they raised their voices in speech, the people understood them. They knew how to reach the popular heart, for the salient experiences of local, civil, and national life (all of which were indissolubly bound up with the religious), were had in common by Prophet and Burgher. The language of the former, accordingly, was that of the latter. It involved the by-words, the maxims, the figures, the symbols, that were in vogue, as well as constant allusions to places, persons, events, which were constantly before the eyes or in the ears of all. Dr. Nevin was not pre-ordained to be a man for the people. We believe that he would have rejoiced in exercising ability of this kind, and that he looked with something like envy upon those who were in possession of popular gifts. When, appearing before the massive assembly gathered in the venerable Tulpehocken church to hear him preach in German, he told his hearers that he was about to preach to them on a text in "*Johannis Evángeljum*," how glad would he have been if he could have proclaimed to that honest and truth-loving people the plain facts of the Gospel with the same simplicity, directness and unction with which God endowed many of our fathers, his co-laborers, and in which some of their German-preaching sons do not come short.

But this was not Dr. Nevin's sphere. His vocation was of a different kind. Still a preacher of the Gospel he would be. And how he preached almost until the end, the reader has an opportunity of learning in the body of this book. But to be a witness-bearer for Christ—this was his vocation, and this he

the Way, and the Life! Put your seal, in the way of a living self-witness, to the truth of God—then will you be prepared for the great work of reconciliation. The ministry of Jesus Christ, in the true and proper sense, is not merely a study or a preaching of doctrine; it is not theological speculation: it is putting the seal to God's word by a personal, living exhibition of the truth."

was destined to become, in a degree of eminence reached by few in this broad land of ours.

Dr. Nevin's mind was so constituted as to fit him to be a leader of thought. Leaders of thought are not generally understood at first. So with those who produce what is epoch-making and original in other spheres, for example, that of art. Beethoven's music and Wordsworth's poetry is becoming intelligible to the greatest mass of those who are musically or poetically inclined, but by degrees. Dr. Nevin's mind naturally turned to fundamental principles, abstract questions and the like. Most persons have a disrelish for matters of this kind; and even the learned are beginning to tell us that speculation may have been a useful occupation in the past, but that its work is done, and what the present and future generations have to concern themselves about is facts.

Dr. Nevin's lot was cast in a most momentous period of the history of the Christian Church. No one felt this more deeply than himself. He compared the situation to the breaking up of the fountains of the great deep. And many great minds agreed with him, and do still agree. A recent English theologian, in a work widely read, says that the crisis now at hand is of more significance than the Reformation of the Sixteenth century.* The reason is that that conflict was confined chiefly to the world of *morals;* whilst the present one covers the world of thought. The leaders of that day raised up their voice against the old church because it had fallen away from the pure life of the early Christians; the agitators of the present are assaulting the church because, they say, it has all along been advocating tenets which are contrary to *reason.*

A man of Dr. Nevin's active mind and broad observation soon opened his eyes to all that the situation involved. Like a Hebrew prophet, concerned above all things for the safety of the ark of Jehovah, his heart was filled with anxiety, and his spirit was agitated within him. He keenly observed the

---

* "Lux Mundi."

gathering phalanxes of the enemy; but he was none the less watchful as to the condition of things in the Church's own camp. Was all right here? He had reason to fear. If weak points are seen, these must be attended to before the enemy can be successfully coped with. He thinks he has discovered some. He brings to bear upon them all the light which a great student of God's Word, and of Church history, like himself, could command. With the utmost candor and sincerity of purpose he makes bold to indicate them. At once the cry was raised from all sides, "An enemy in the camp!" He stood his ground like a hero. He went back to the sources of history, and sounded the depths of modern learning. He employed all the arguments, marshalled the authorities, and utilized his vast dialectic skill, to convince all who would listen that his view of the state of the case was correct. The only policy, as he tried to point out, which could insure success, was that of holding fast to what was absolutely vital and essential on our side (for example, the fundamental facts of the Gospel as set forth in the Apostles' Creed), and at the same time yielding to the foe what it could rightly call its own (for example, the legitimate results of strictly scientific research, although they might conflict with the literal sense of the Sacred Scriptures).* Some said, "You want to carry us back to Rome;" others said, "By your rationalism you want to take us directly across to the enemy's ground."

Few men of God, during the present century, have been so

---

* "In the meantime, to all practical intents and purposes, the whole cause of what was once considered to be the *inspiration* of the Old Testament, was allowed to lapse quietly into a sort of pious myth, much like the inspiration of Homer with the Greeks. Any real divine life, then, there may ever have been in it, fairly smothered out of it now by the preponderance assigned everywhere to its *outward letter*. This is made to be the great battle-field, accordingly, for an endless war between the Bible and secular science; where the champions of the Bible are sure to come off always second best, because fighting, in truth, always on the same side with their naturalistic opponents."—*Mer. Rev.*, 1878, p. 33.

rudely denounced and decried as was Dr. Nevin. His followers had to bear reproach with him; and of course the church also, in whose institutions he was stationed as a teacher, and of which he will always be regarded as the bright and shining light. He was ever ready to withdraw, and at times did withdraw, as if to say, "I will bear the shame alone;" but the Church, through her highest judicatory, always said "No. We endorse your course, and say to you, Work and teach according to the dictates of your conscience, and the responsibility is ours." He never sought position, nor honor, nor gold. It was the cause of truth that was the object of his concern. Of Dr. Nevin it can ever be said, as it can be of but few men, he was not governed by the dictates of the flesh, but by those of the Spirit.

From the nature of the case it is evident what the character of his literary productions would be. The slur has been cast upon him that he was "nothing if not polemical." How much ignorance is betrayed by such a remark! How could it be otherwise? Then, too, all his discussions turned upon what lay deep down below the surface of the current literature of the day. Besides this, the character of his work in the college and Seminary rendered it necessary to move in a line of study and labor upon which only more advanced scholars enter. His style is accordingly not that of a writer for the people; and much of what he has written can be appreciated only by those who have time and inclination to follow closely in similar pursuits.*

---

* Is there not something pathetic in language like the following in which he seems to bewail as an infirmity his inability to make his thoughts clear to the mind of the general reader? "It seems to us *exhausting*, even to the extent of spiritual deliquium, only to think of such a thing (namely, the idea that there is nothing more in the Bible than what 'thought or speech can compass in their natural human form'). Not without some sense of such fainting in our spirit, therefore, we leave the subject here for the present. And we will add also, not without some inward resonance of that mournful complaint of the ancient Jewish prophet, 'Ah, Lord God!

In the sermons that follow the reader has the opportunity of becoming better acquainted with this eminent servant of God. They appear in a form which makes his deep thoughts, indeed, his profound inner experience, in a measure accessible to all.

They were delivered at a most interesting period of his history. There was a time when he thought it was necessary, in view of the looseness of view prevailing on subjects connected with the church, her authority, her sacraments, her hallowed forms of worship, to insist with stress and emphasis upon what was objective and historical. We might say, respect for properly constituted authority was the ruling principle of his life. But later in his career it dawned upon him that there were questions connected with the claims of the Scriptures to be the inspired word of God, which had been in a measure overlooked by him.* More than ever does he become convinced that the living Christ, once crucified, but now exalted upon His throne in glory, speaks to men out of and through the Bible. Men do not know what a storehouse

they say of me, 'DOTH HE NOT SPEAK PARABLES?'' "—Close of sermon on "The Bread of Life."

"I have endeavored to show in my article *Christ* the *Inspiration of His Own Word* (GOD KNOWS WITH WHAT OPPRESSIVE SENSE OF WEAKNESS), (italics ours), the transcendent significance of the MAN CHRIST JESUS in the economy of the world's redemption." From the last of Dr. Nevin's published writings.—*Review*, 1883, p. 13.

* " In our past controversies with regard to baptism and the Lord's Supper, we may not have done justice always to what must be considered in this way the true and real pre-eminence of the Word above all sacraments. In contending for the faith delivered to the saints in regard to the sacraments, we may have failed to intone properly what the presence of the LORD in his WORD means, without which there is no room to conceive of his presence among men in any other form. Should this have been so, let us trust that it may be so no longer; while we unite mind and heart in seeking an understanding of divine inspiration better than that which now too commonly prevails, and join, one and all, on bended knee, in daily prayer, 'Open thou mine eyes, O Lord, that I may behold wondrous things out of thy law.' "—*Mercersburg Review*, 1879, p. 29.

of heavenly treasure is here at hand.* Especially in these days is the value of the Old Testament underestimated.† In so far as his teaching had fallen short in the past, with God's help he would make that right. In his later writings he falls into a mode of expression more obscure and recondite than ever. Even his preaching was said to be in an unknown tongue.

These sermons fall in what may be called a transition period. They are characterized by marked moderation and clearness. They are free from the polemical, the speculative and mystical elements elsewhere to be found. The topics are varied. The plain facts of Scripture and truths of the Gospel are presented

---

* "They are oracles of God; not dead, but living; not dumb, but as the voice of seven thunders sounding from heaven. Such only is the miraculous constitution of the Bible, by which, in boundless difference from all worldly philosophy and science, it is found to be a real medium of communication between men on earth and angels in heaven, bringing all together as one new creation in Christ Jesus."—*Review*, 1882, p. 41.

† "The Decalogue, we have already said, underlies the universal structure of the Old Testament revelation, distinguished as 'the Law of Moses, the Prophets and the Psalms;' and the quality of its inspired origination out of heaven from God, as we have now considered it, is to be regarded then as extending into every part and portion of that revelation; making the whole to be what is to be understood by the Word of God. The Jewish history, the Jewish commonwealth, the Jewish civil institutions and laws, so far as they are brought forward in the Bible, the Jewish ritual in all its details, come alike under the supernatural character and rule. So it is with every one of the psalms; and so it is also with all the prophets. . . .

"And so we might go on indefinitely; but here we stop for the present. It is enough for the object of this article, if it may serve only in a general way to establish, from the demonstration of the Holy Ghost in the Word itself, the truth of the angelic thesis, *The testimony of Jesus is the spirit of prophecy*. That means necessarily, as we have seen, that the self-witnessing power of the Lord's life actually lives in the Holy Scriptures, as their animating spirit or soul, so that it may be said of them universally, as of the ark of old, JEHOVAH IS THERE. *How* that great wonder can be—the 'flame of fire out of the midst of a bush, and yet the bush not consumed' —is another question, going deep into the doctrine of God and the science of the human mind. But the first thing needed here, as in all the mysteries

in a simple and practical way. They are helps to devotion, supports to faith, and words of comfort to heavy hearts.

If any one wishes to learn more of the character and life of Dr. Nevin, of his pious boyhood and student life, his brilliant career as Professor in the Presbyterian Seminary at Allegheny, of his sacrifice in accepting the call to the obscure and humble school of the prophets at our own Mercersburg, of his self-denying labors and heart-cutting tribulations there, of the vicissitudes that followed, especially of his heroic devotion to the church, to the cause of the truth, to the interests of the many faithful pupils still honoring his memory, of his martyr-like patience, and of his Patmos-like retirement, where, as St. John, he lived in the realities of the spiritual world,* he may find all in the two works written by loving spiritual sons, who in this way have laid garlands of fragrance upon his grave.

"*Almighty God, with whom do live the spirits of those who depart hence in the Lord, and with whom the souls of the faith-*

---

of Christianity, is full heaven-wrought persuasion of the reality of the fact itself, which is thus made to challenge any such deeper study (Matt. xvi. 17). Where that persuasion of faith is wanting, as with men commonly, all pretended farther study of the subject can never come to more than a helpless, self-reliant floundering of the understanding in the asphaltic sea of naturalism—the burial-place of Sodom and her sister cities of the Plain."—*Mercersburg Review*, 1877, p. 212.

* "The morning star is to be a recompense of that purity which is the fundamental requirement of the whole epistle. According to 2 Pet. 1: 19, the *morning star* symbolizes the full dawn of the New Testament day. According to Rev. 22: 16, Christ on the way of His speedy Advent is the bright Morning-star. The promise, therefore, is that the pure and unadulterated Christian as a victor over fanaticisms (*i. e.*, wild and spurious forms of Christian life, whether hierarchical or sectarian), shall, in advance of others, behold the morning-star of the new time, the last time, the Coming of the Lord, as if that morning-star were his own; nay, he shall even point to the morning-star as the object of his prophecy. He shall stand 'in the morning radiance of eternity, in the full enjoyment of Christian hope, Christian progress, the true ante-celebration of the Coming of Christ.'"—*Lange on Rev. 2: 28.*

ful, after they are delivered from the burden of the flesh, are in joy and felicity; we give Thee hearty thanks for the good examples of all those Thy servants, who, having finished their course in faith, do now rest from their labors. And we beseech Thee, that we, with all those who are departed in the true faith of Thy holy name, may have our perfect consummation and bliss, both in body and soul, in Thy eternal and everlasting glory; through Jesus Christ our Lord. Amen."

CONTENTS.

SERMON I.

The Second Sunday in Advent.
"THE DAY-SPRING FROM ON HIGH."

St. Luke xxi. 25–33.

" And there shall be signs in the sun, and in the moon, and in the stars; and upon the earth distress of nations, with perplexity; the sea and the waves roaring; men's hearts failing them for fear, and for looking after those things which are coming on the earth; for the powers of heaven shall be shaken." . . . . page 35

SERMON II.

The First Sunday after The Epiphany.
THE SELF-AUTHENTICATING POWER OF THE TRUTH.

St. Luke ii. 41–52.

" Now His parents went to Jerusalem every year at the feast of the Passover. And when He was twelve years old, they went up to Jerusalem after the custom of the feast." . . . . page 43

SERMON III.

The Second Sunday after The Epiphany.
"THE VICTORY OVER THE WORLD."

St. Matthew xiv. 22–33.

" And straightway Jesus constrained His disciples to get into a ship, and to go before Him unto the other side, while He sent the multitudes away." . . . . page 52

SERMON IV.

The Fourth Sunday after The Epiphany.

THE PRECIOUSNESS OF FAITH.

2 Peter i. 1.

"*Simon Peter, a servant and an apostle of Jesus Christ, to them that have obtained like precious faith with us through the righteousness of God and our Saviour Jesus Christ.*" . . . . page 60

SERMON V.

The Sixth Sunday after The Epiphany.

JESUS THE ONLY MEDIATOR.

John i. 51.

"*And he saith unto them, Verily, verily I say unto you, Hereafter ye shall see heaven open, and the angels of God ascending and descending on the Son of Man.*" . . . . page 69

SERMON VI.

The Sunday before Lent—Quinquagesima.

THE LAW OF SPIRITUAL VISION.

Matthew vi. 22-23.

"*The light of the body is the eye: if therefore thine eye be single, thy whole body shall be full of light. But if thine eye be evil, thy whole body shall be full of darkness. If therefore the light that is in thee be darkness, how great is that darkness!*" . . . . page 79

SERMON VII.

The Third Sunday in Lent.

HELP FROM ABOVE.

Psalm cxxx. v. 1.

"*Out of the depths have I cried unto Thee, O Lord.*" . . . . page 87

SERMON VIII.

The Fourth Sunday in Lent.
THE WAY OF THE TRANSGRESSOR.
Proverbs xiii. 15.

"*The way of transgressors is hard.*" . . . . page 96

SERMON IX.

The Sixth Sunday in Lent—Palm Sunday.
SUFFERING AND REIGNING.
Philippians ii. 5–11.

"*Let this mind be in you, which was also in Christ Jesus: who, being in the form of God, thought it not robbery to be equal with God; but made himself of no reputation, and took upon him the form of a servant, and was made in the likeness of men; and being found in fashion as a man, he humbled himself, and became obedient unto death, even the death of the cross.*" . . . . . page 101

SERMON X.

The First Sunday after Easter.
"THE GLORIOUS PRINCE OF SALVATION."
Hebrews ii. 10.

"*For it became him, for whom are all things, and by whom are all things, in bringing many sons unto glory, to make the captain of their salvation perfect through sufferings.*" . . . . . . page 108

SERMON XI.

The Second Sunday after Easter.
SEEING THE FATHER.
John xiv. 9.

"*Jesus saith unto him, Have I been so long time with you, and yet hast thou not known me, Philip? He that hath seen me, hath seen the Father; and how sayest thou then, Shew us the Father?*" . . . . page 114

SERMON XII.

The Fifth Sunday after Easter.

THE BELIEVER'S CROWN OF LIFE.

Revelation iii. 11.

"*Behold, I come quickly: hold that fast which thou hast, that no man take thy crown.*" . . . . page 122

SERMON XIII.

Ascension Day.

THE SIGNIFICANCE OF THE FORTY DAYS.

Acts i. 9.

"*And when he had spoken these things, while they beheld, he was taken up; and a cloud received him out of their sight.*" . . page 128

SERMON XIV.

The Fourteenth Sunday after Trinity.

OBEDIENCE THE WAY TO A KNOWLEDGE OF THE TRUTH.

John vii. 17.

"*If any man will do his will, he shall know of the doctrine, whether it be of God, or whether I speak of myself.*" . . . . page 133

SERMON XV.

The Nineteenth Sunday after Trinity.

THE KNOWLEDGE OF GOD THROUGH CHRIST ALONE.

Matthew xi. 27.

"*All things are delivered unto me of my Father: and no man knoweth the Son but the Father: neither knoweth any man the Father save the Son, and he to whomsoever the Son will reveal him.*" . page 140

SERMON XVI.

The Twentieth Sunday after Trinity.

THE GOSPEL FOR THE POOR.

Luke vii. 22.

"*To the poor the Gospel is preached.*" . . . . page 146

SERMON XVII.

The Twentieth Sunday after Trinity.

CHRIST THE ONLY SATISFYING PORTION OF THE SOUL.

Matthew xi. 28-30.

"*Come unto me, all ye that labor and are heavy laden, and I will give you rest.*" . . . . page 153

SERMON XVIII.

The Twenty-Third Sunday after Trinity.

SEARCHING THE SCRIPTURES.

John v. 39-40.

"*Search the Scriptures; for in them ye think ye have eternal life, and they are they which testify of me.*" . . . . page 162

SERMON XIX.

The Fourth Sunday before Advent.

THE UNBROKEN COMMUNION OF THE SAINTS.

Matthew ix. 18-26.

"*While he spake these things unto them, behold there came a certain ruler, and worshipped him, saying, My daughter is even now dead; but come and lay thy hand upon her, and she shall live.*" . . . . page 167

SERMON XX.

The Third Sunday before Advent.

THE PERSON OF CHRIST THE CENTRAL OBJECT OF FAITH.

John vi. 28–29.

"*Then said they unto him, What shall we do, that we might work the works of God? Jesus answered and said unto them, This is the work of God, that ye believe on him whom he hath sent.*" . . . . page 175

SERMON XXI.

The Second Sunday before Advent.

THE VOICE OF WISDOM.

Proverbs viii. 1–10.

"*Doth not Wisdom cry? and Understanding put forth her voice? She standeth in the top of the high places, by the way in the places of the paths. She crieth at the gates, at the entry of the city, at the coming in at the doors: Unto you, O men, I call, and my voice is to the sons of man.*" . . . . page 183

SERMON XXII.

The Sunday before Advent.

THE SECOND COMING OF OUR LORD.

2 Peter iii. 3–14.

"*Knowing this first, that there shall come in the last days scoffers, walking after their own lusts, and saying, Where is the promise of his coming?*" . . . . page 189

SERMON XXIII.

The Sunday before Advent.

THE SECOND COMING OF OUR LORD.

2 Peter iii. 10-14.

"*But this day of the Lord will come as a thief in the night; in the which the heavens shall pass away with a great noise, and the elements shall melt with fervent heat, the earth also and the works that are therein shall be burned up.*" . . . . page 194

SERMON XXIV.

A Baccalaureate Sermon.

NATURE AND GRACE.

John iii. 13.

"*No man hath ascended up to heaven, but he that came down from heaven, even the Son of man which is in heaven.*" . . . . page 201

COLLEGE CHAPEL SERMONS.

The Second Sunday in Advent.

THE DAY-SPRING FROM ON HIGH.

The Gospel Lesson for the Day.—St. Luke xxi. 25–33.

"*And there shall be signs in the sun, and in the moon, and in the stars; and upon the earth distress of nations, with perplexity; the sea and the waves roaring; men's hearts failing them for fear, and for looking after those things which are coming on the earth; for the powers of heaven shall be shaken.*"

It may seem strange, at first sight, that a passage of this kind should have been selected for our reading and meditation during the season of Advent, which has for its theme the appearing of Christ in the flesh. One might rather expect that the Scripture lessons for this season of the Church Year would be of a more cheerful tone, that they would partake more than they do of the general character of joy expressed in the song of the angels to the shepherds on the plains of Bethlehem, announcing "good tidings of great joy which shall be to all people."

On the contrary our attention is called away in an apparently different direction altogether, not to the beginning of the Christian religion, but to its consummation and end, the mind being invited by the lessons appointed for our reading to the consideration of that state of the world in which the heavens and the earth are regarded as being in commotion as a sure and certain prognostication of the coming of the Son of Man, just as the bursting of the buds on the trees in the springtime is an unfailing harbinger of the coming summer.

The propriety of the selections, however, appears when we consider the close and intimate relation existing between the first advent of our Lord in the flesh and His second advent in the clouds of heaven; and particularly when we reflect upon that profound and universal law, the operation of which we observe everywhere, in the physical quite as well as in the ethical world—that law according to which darkness must ever go before light, danger must ever precede deliverance.

The first coming of our Lord in His incarnation brings into view this deep fundamental law that holds everywhere in the constitution of the world. We see the operation of this law in nature, considered even as standing apart from the gospel. We look on nature as manifesting itself in different systems, the one outward, the other inward. There is a necessary original connection between the two, as there always is between darkness and light, sorrow and joy, labor and rest, tribulation and glory. The latter state cannot come in any case except through its preceding opposite condition. There is no light unless darkness precedes. This great law forces itself on the conviction of all men universally, even amongst the heathen. The heathen philosophy saw full well, by the natural reason, and without the aid of revelation, that the path of freedom was and always must be the path of self-denial. The Stoic philosophers especially acknowledged this fact, in opposition to the teachings of Epicurus, which they knew could tend only to moral defeat and death. They knew full well that if anything like life and freedom were to be attained by the human spirit, it must be by the renunciation of the world. If man is ever to pass up into a higher life the laws and powers of the lower world now about him must be subdued and overcome.

It is in harmony with this law that our Saviour says, "If any man will be my disciple, let him deny himself and take up his cross and follow me;" let him renounce the world and meet tribulation, and so shall he find peace and joy, according to that promise, "If any man serve me, let him follow me, and where I am, there shall also my servant be." We meet the same law everywhere in the declarations of our Saviour—"What shall it profit a man, if he shall gain the whole world, and lose his own soul:" "Whosoever will save his life shall lose it; but whosoever shall lose his life for my sake and the gospel's the same shall save it;" and those words of comfort to His disciples on the eve of His departure out of the world—"Ye shall weep and lament, but the world shall rejoice; and ye shall be sorrowful, but your sorrow shall be turned into joy."

This same law which thus operates in the higher kingdom of grace and in the moral world is revealed in the constitution of nature universally, and is felt and acknowledged by all men—the law that requires that darkness should precede light. And we are prepared thus to see how necessary it was that darkness should precede the coming of Christ, who is the true light of the world. In one view, indeed, all that is great, high and glorious, especially all advancement that has been reached in the progress of history, is typical of the coming of Christ—of His first coming as well as of His second (for the two are indissolubly conjoined); but it is also true that the dark side of our existence involves a promise or pledge that the Son of Man shall come. This promise lies in the conception of the order to which we have adverted, first darkness then light, first labor then rest, first tribulation then joy. Between these two there is a necessary, natural, original relation. All pain and sorrow carry in them a promise of something good to come, not in the way merely of fancy or imagination, but by reason of the fixed and settled constitution of the world. As we say, "The darkest hour is just before the dawn," so in the moral world, the darkest times of the world's life are the surest pledges of the coming of Christ in glory.

We meet a verification of this in a broad and general view of history. Previous to the coming of Christ the times were dark. Undoubtedly there was a large amount of progress amongst the Greeks and Romans, as well as in the world at large for four thousand years, in a moral, social, and even in a religious sense. But so far as there had been any gain in any of these directions, it must be regarded only as reaching out toward the full truth. The promise of help and relief for the world's life at that stage of its progress, however, lay not in its apparently hopeful achievements, but rather quite in the opposite direction. In the dark side of that old world-life, in the failures of that old-world history, we see a deeper prophecy and proof of the coming of Christ than in all these relative exhibitions of progress. For always, in that old world, along side of such gain and advancement, there was a continual progress in failure and defeat, showing more and more, as time moved on, that the powers of our human nature are inefficient to bring about the redemption of the world. That long experiment of four thousand years showed clearly enough that the world was defeated, and foiled in its hope of attaining by its own power what its consciousness demanded. And the prophecy of the coming of Christ was strong right here on this dark side. When all the efforts of the world had been pushed to their extremest limits, the world was still sunk hopelessly in the abyss of its misery. Then it was that it pleased God to reveal Himself in the coming of Christ.

We see thus that the religious failures of the old world prepared the way for Christ. The old systems, on which men relied, were foiled, shorn of their power and shown to be a delusion. We can thus see how the failures of the old world revealed the necessity for the coming of Christ. And it is only in this way that we are at all prepared to understand the long delay in human history prior to the coming of Christ. Why, it may be asked, did God wait so long before sending His Son into the world? Why should four thousand years of human struggle, failure and misery have been allowed slowly and wearily to pass away? Why did He not send His Son into the world in the time of Noah, or Abraham, or Jeremiah? Because certain failures in the course of human history were absolutely necessary to make His coming at all intelligible to men.

The relation which the sorrow and suffering of that old world bore to the coming of Christ, continues to hold good now in the life of the world at large, as well as in the experience of every individual man. Sorrow and affliction are followed by the coming of Christ by His Spirit, as He Himself promised, "I will not leave you orphans; I will come unto you." These straits and exigencies of Christian life and experience are comings, continual comings of Christ to His people. Christ comes to His Church still as He came to His disciples on the sea of Galilee, for that occasion may be considered as typical and symbolical of the Christian life. In the midst of the darkness and tempest on the sea of life Christ comes to us with reassuring words, "It is I; be not afraid." So, too, in the Church at large. Christ always comes to resuscitate the expiring life of man. So long as men are at home in the world, so long are they unprepared for the coming of Christ. The man who feels at home in the outward conditions of health, strength and prosperity, cannot see Christ, cannot receive Him. "They that are whole need not a physician." Christ came not "to call the righteous, but sinners to repentance." There must be a sense of sickness, and this is often accompanied by a breaking up of the outward circumstances of prosperity. Before Christ can come to any man that man must feel his need, just as the disciples on the sea of Galilee felt theirs. So it is universally. When men feel their need, are in extremity, know not which way else to turn, and have their vision unsealed, as it were, the scales dropping from their eyes, then they are in condition to receive Christ; then do they begin to cry out, as Peter of old, "Lord, if it be thou, bid me come to thee on the water."

Therefore we should not at all wonder that, at this season of Advent, in the lessons appointed for our reading and meditation, sorrow and joy are so closely conjoined. The language employed in the Gospel lesson for the day is more or less metaphorical, but the outward signs here spoken of will, no doubt, accompany our Lord's second coming, although, as we all know, these signs are primarily applicable to the destruction of

Jerusalem, as is seen in our Lord's declaration, "This generation shall not pass away till all be fulfilled."

All this seems to be an argument against the popular supposition that the coming of Christ will be the result of the easy onflowing of natural forces and powers already in the world; that the progress now going on in the social and political world, in art and science and literature, in the subjection of nature to the power of man, will eventually reach such a lofty stage of advancement as to usher in the millenium. Is not that the purpose for which Christ came into the world? I am afraid not. All this progress and advancement may be a sign and assurance in one of those two ways in which the coming of the Lord may be foreshadowed or prophesied, (as we saw a moment ago), the partial and relative good possible to human endeavor witnessing always, certainly, to the perfect and absolute; but such a view of human history and development as contemplates the millennium as possible to human effort, and as being the efflorescence of it, overlooks that great and fundamental, universal law operating in the profoundest depths of man's moral, social and religious nature—this namely, that darkness must precede the light. No doubt we are in advance of the times that are past; but it seems unreasonable to suppose that these victories of a merely natural kind in the organization of the social and political world, will ever usher in the millennium. They did not bring in the first advent, and they will not bring in the second. When we have reached our highest possible advancement, only the coming of Christ will solve the problem. The deeper and more positive prophecy of the coming of Christ will no doubt be found at last in the helpless misery of humanity. Still side by side with the defeat and misery of our life, under one aspect, will go its progress under another, so that we can truly look for the coming of the Son of Man when all around is progress and when we seem to be approaching the highest possible perfection in the social and political world.

There is a close inward connection between our sorrows and the coming of Christ, although we may not be able to see how this can be. As only darkness can reveal the starry world above us, so also only darkness can reveal to us the heavenly world from the depths of our own moral and spiritual nature. There is thus a close connection between the cross and the crown, and if our eyes were only opened that we could see, if our apprehension of spiritual things were only clear and strong, then should we regard all of life's sorrows and burdens as being, in the truest sense, blessings.

December 5th, 1869.

The First Sunday after The Epiphany.

THE SELF-AUTHENTICATING POWER OF THE TRUTH.

The Gospel Lesson for the Day.—St. Luke ii. 41–52.

"Now His parents went to Jerusalem every year at the feast of the Passover. And when He was twelve years old, they went up to Jerusalem after the custom of the feast."

THE mediatorial work of our Saviour completes itself in His resurrection and ascension. Between His incarnation and His resurrection His divine human life was steadily unfolding itself in the way of a gradual progress. This progressive development in the life of the God-Man may be regarded as an Epiphany, which may be contemplated either as a whole or under a narrower aspect. The Epiphany may be taken as referring to His birth alone, for example, or it may be extended so as to cover His whole life from beginning to end; and even under the narrower view, it may be regarded as comprehending several successive stages, more or less clearly defined. When we examine these lessons assigned for our reading during the Epiphany season, we see that there is a close internal connexion between them. First we have the visit of the wise men, then the appearance of the Saviour in the temple at the age of twelve years, and next the manifestation of His glory in the beginning of miracles at Cana. It is not by accident that such a progress is observable in these lessons, but the selection has evidently been made with the wisest design; for there plainly was such a progress in the Epiphany of our Saviour's life, beginning with His birth and reaching on with unbroken continuity, and with increasing fulness and power, to His final glorification when He sat down at the right hand of God. Even before the full opening of His own ministry, the Epiphany had already commenced in the preaching of John the Baptist, who was enabled to foretell His coming and to point Him out as "The Son of God," by what occurred at His baptism. But, up to the time of the birth of our Saviour, all the events connected with it, although they carried in them an evidence for the divine Messiahship, were yet not enough of themselves to authenticate or make it sure. These events, though necessary as preparing the way for the true Epiphany, or self-manifestation of the Son of God, were largely of an outward or external character. And this self-manifestation of His glory and majesty involves different degrees, or successive stages, advancing continually from the more outward to the more inward in the unfolding of the wonderful life of the God-Man.

First, then, we have the visit of the wise men from the east. The presence of Christ was manifested to them by the star, and then, shortly afterward, to all Jerusalem, by the excitement caused by the slaughter of the Innocents. This was an Epiphany, and one of great force and value so far as it went; still it was largely external, and of one character with all previous evidence of the coming of the Messiah as this was furnished in the preparation for the advent of the Son of God amongst the Jews, and also in that preparation for the same which, as we can now see plainly enough, existed amongst the heathen. In both the Jewish and the Gentile world there was a manifestation or an Epiphany of the Messiah, His Advent making itself felt in the world long before it came actually to pass, in that wonderful preparation which was plainly going forward for many centuries, in a negative way amongst the heathen, in a positive way amongst God's chosen people, the Jews. In both cases that preparation was an evidence of His coming, as it was indeed in a profound sense an Epiphany of the Son of God in history.

Now, the star in the east and the visit of the wise men belong to this kind of evidence, being yet, however, something more; for here was a miracle, nature testifying to the presence of her Lord. In this there is something exceeding all previous evidence; yet, at the same time, it is of the same general quality or character as the former, being something relatively outward, external; an evidence for the presence of the Lord of all coming from beyond and not emanating from His own person; and therefore lacking the power fully to authenticate His presence and power in the world. Had there been no evidence besides, this of itself would not have been sufficient to produce in the minds of men such a conviction of the presence in the world of the Lord of all as to leave men without excuse. There must be something more, and something more convincing; an evidence arising from within, not from without the mystery of the Word made flesh—a breathing forth, a shining out from His own majestic personal presence. Without this kind of evidence, the fact of His being in the world could not have been authenticated in any other way—not by the world of nature, not by the world of history; for it was a supernatural fact, and must of necessity be authenticated by an outshining, by an outstreaming of its own glory.

We say, then, that the conception of the Epiphany requires that the evidence of what the Saviour was must proceed from His own person. We can see this plainly enough, for instance, in the events connected with our Saviour's baptism. In order that John the Baptist should be certain concerning the Messiah, it was not enough that he should know the Saviour personally, or should be fully acquainted with the Scriptures bearing upon the nature and office of Him that was to come—he must have another kind of evidence, an evidence proceeding directly and immediately from the person and presence of the Christ Himself; as we see on the day of our Saviour's baptism, when John "looked upon Jesus as He walked, and said, ' Behold the Lamb of God!'"

For this reason it is that the festival of the Epiphany cannot stop short with an account merely of the visit of the wise men. We have a number of sundays after the Epiphany, each with its lesson of some particular aspect of the manifestation of our Saviour's power and glory, there being in the Epiphany season, considered as a whole, a steady progress or gradual advancement in the development of its underlying idea. There was, evidently, in the life of our Saviour such a progressive unfolding or development. The exhibition of our Saviour's divine presence was not full and complete at first. It would not have been a true human life had it been so. We are not to suppose that the presence of the divine nature of Christ was a uniform fact either for Himself or for the world. It was not of a uniform character throughout, but submitted to the necessary law of a gradual unfolding or development. There was a process or a progress analogous to the regular unfolding of our own human life, involving a profound mystery which we cannot at all fathom.

This fact is brought into view in the passage of Scripture which constitutes our text—the appearance of our

Saviour in the temple at twelve years of age. He had grown up as an obedient member of the family of Joseph and Mary without revealing His own nature to others—and we must go even further than this, and say that He Himself was not fully conscious of His own nature, or His infancy would have been mere magic. There is no attempt in the Gospel narrative to emphasize His divine nature unduly, or to press its claims out of all proportion to the demands of the human nature which He had assumed. The evangelical record does not portray Him, for instance, as having performed a single miracle during His infancy, as has been done in the so-called apocryphal gospels which have come down to us, written by some who were no doubt eager enough to magnify the Saviour's power and glory. Instead, however, of doing this, these spurious, and often frivolous, narratives greatly detract therefrom. There is such a striking contrast between the miracles attributed to our Saviour in these false gospels and those which are narrated in the evangelical record that, to one looking at the matter rightly, there is in this very contrast one of the most clear, powerful and convincing arguments for the truth of the life of our Saviour as portrayed by the Canonical gospels. Had this wonderful life been a mere fiction, or an ingenious contrivance of man, the narrative never could have escaped such spurious and grotesque miracles as these. The more we compare the two, the one with the other, the more we contrast them, the more are we convinced and shut up to the conclusion that this is as certainly the true as that is certainly the false.

In the Lesson for the Day we have the only notice that is taken of the childhood of Jesus. At the age of twelve years the Jewish children made a public profession of their faith, and this occasion in the life of a Jewish boy is, with singular propriety, chosen as the occasion of a perfect dramatic scene in the life of our Saviour. It is something very difficult to select one event in a life of thirty years with a view to making it the subject of a dramatic scene. Had any uninspired writer attempted this in giving an account of the life of our Saviour, this would have been the inevitable result—there would have been more than enough. In this view of the case, the scene set before us in the Gospel Lesson is a perfect picture, a triumph of dramatic art.

Our Saviour, here, is absorbed in hearing the learned doctors of the law, and in asking them questions, not to embarrass or confuse them certainly, but in perfectly good faith, His questions proceeding from a sincere and earnest childlike heart. He sat at the feet of the doctors desiring information and seeking to be instructed. His parents, as they went down from Jerusalem toward their own home, missing Him in the company, returned, and after three days, or on the third day, found Him thus situated, and asked with some tone of gentle reproof, "Why hast thou thus dealt with us?" a purely parental and altogether natural inquiry. He answered, "How is it that ye sought me? Wist ye not that I must be about my Father's business?" Then He obediently went down with them, and subject to them grew up to the full stature of manhood, His human life unfolding itself in an entirely natural and normal way in conjunction with His divine nature.

This passage in the life of the Saviour is thus seen to involve an Epiphany far beyond that of the visit of the wise men, for it was a manifestation from Himself, an evidence given out from His own consciousness. It was more inward than the other, deeper far, and made itself felt as something full of majesty; for "all were astonished at His understanding and answers," even the doctors and His parents. "But his mother kept all these sayings in her heart."

His Epiphany, however, by no means ends here. His whole subsequent life is an Epiphany—a shining forth of the power, majesty and grace of His divine-human personality. But there are in the Gospel narrative certain grand and striking occasions of such a manifestation—occasions when His life displayed or revealed itself in a special way, and in a degree far above what was common. In the Gospel Lesson for the next Lord's Day, the Second Sunday after the Epiphany, we have a sublime illustration of this, in the miracle of the water turned into wine. "This beginning of miracles did Jesus in Cana of Galilee, and manifested forth his glory"—even inanimate, physical nature being made, in a manner in keeping with its own constitution, to testify to the presence and power of the Lord of all. The fact of His being in the world was indeed witnessed by the star in the east, but in this case nature, instead of merely testifying to His presence in an external and outward way, depends on Him, the Creator of all, and yields itself the medium for the shining out of His great glory. Nature was here, as it were, etherealized in its own order, water passing up into wine. The significance of the miracle consists largely in this lifting up, this sublimation of nature; for it was shown in this, the first of all our Saviour's miracles, that the old world of nature, suffering under the curse of sin, was not only brought under His power in an external way, but was so transfused by the power of His life as to render a resurrection and glorification possible and certain. His power over nature is further shown in the selections of Scripture appointed for the following Epiphany Sundays — in healing the sick, in stilling the tempest on the sea, and in that marvelous manifestation of His unspeakable glory on the Mount of Transfiguration.

It is to be observed and carefully noted that the whole Epiphany of Christ is its own argument. This does not mean that every other kind of evidence is excluded, as being of no account. All such evidence as is drawn, for instance, from ancient history—both Jewish and Pagan—as a preparation for the coming of Christ, has its proper place and must be accorded its just weight, but is not of itself sufficient to authenticate Christ. So it is with all the Christian evidences, as they are called. They have their importance and their significance. If they had been wanting, we should lack the evidence that Christ had come, for they must accompany such a fact, though not of themselves sufficient to authenticate or to establish it. We cannot prove Christianity by miracles or by prophecy. We cannot prove it to an unbeliever in that way; no, nor even to ourselves. "Even though one should rise from the dead," men would not, for that reason alone, believe. Such a conviction must be the direct and immediate result of a divine light from a divine life breaking in upon us. The design of the Gospel of St. John is just this—to set before us the birth, life, death—in a word, the whole Epiphany of Christ; so that we are shut up to the irresistible conclusion that this was the Son of God. Not that we are to make no account of any other evidence—such evidence can indeed prepare the way to such a conviction—but if not accompanied or followed by that other, higher, self-authenticating power of the Truth, it must and will surely fail of that authority and weight which it otherwise might have.

We can see how important it is for us to know this in our own experience, to keep this kind of evidence before us continually, and to allow Christ to bear witness for Himself to our own spirits. In proportion as we do this will the glorious Epiphany of the Son of Man be found to break in upon us with its own overwhelming power, causing us to exclaim with St. Peter, "Thou art the Christ, the Son of the living God!"—causing us to exclaim, in the language of the people to the Samaritan woman, "Now we believe, not because of thy saying: for we have heard him ourselves, and know that this indeed is the Christ, the Saviour of the world!"

January 9, 1870.

The Second Sunday after The Epiphany.

THE VICTORY OVER THE WORLD.

St. Matthew xiv. 22-33.

"*And straightway Jesus constrained his disciples to get into a ship, and to go before him unto the other side, while he sent the multitudes away, &c.*"

A LARGE part of the Gospel consists of the parables and miracles of our Lord, which stand in close and intimate relation with each other. The parables result from the correspondence existing between the world of nature and the world of mind, or spirit. The two constitute one system, and have an inward harmony, being governed by one underlying and fundamental law. To the mind of Christ the whole world was a parable. He saw the complete harmony of nature and spirit. His miracles are exhibitions of the power of His higher nature over the world. In both parables and miracles there is, undoubtedly, an inner sense, or spiritual signification, for those who have the eye to see, or the ear to hear, or the understanding to apprehend it.

The occasion to which the text refers is replete with such significance. It is full of comprehensive and wide-reaching instruction. It is a striking picture, in itself regarded, which is here presented for our consideration, and it is still more impressive and grand when we see in it an illustration—a parable, as it were—of moral and spiritual situations, surroundings and experiences; the sea swept by the storm, the waves rolling high, the wind whistling and roaring over the deep, the ship tossed with the waves, the disciples alone and toiling at their oars, the Saviour up in the mountain praying. Seemingly forsaken, overcome by the power of the sea, all hope gone, the disciples are ready to despair. Then, when everything looks darkest and most hopeless, behold the Master comes walking, in calm majesty, over the tossing waters!

Observe the effect His approach produced upon the disciples: "And when the disciples saw him walking on the sea, they were troubled, saying, It is a spirit! and they cried out for fear." For this is the usual feeling of men at the approach of what is, or is supposed to be, a supernatural presence—fear and awe. Then He reassured them, "Be of good cheer: it is I: be not afraid." They knew His voice, and in their simple trust in Him their fears disappeared. Peter, impulsive as ever, requests the Lord to allow him to come to Him on the sea. At the Lord's command he goes down, sees the danger, sinks, cries for help, is rescued. "And when they were come into the ship, the wind ceased. Then they that were in the ship came and worshipped him, saying, Of a truth thou art the Son of God!"

We have here a miracle, indeed, and yet a parable too, and one full of a manifold meaning, which may not well be put into words, yet is felt with power by the pious soul. The miracle may have different explanations, and varying applications, suited to different situations in the life of the individual or in the experience of the Church. But all such applications are embraced in its comprehensive sweep. For our present purpose we may see in it:

I. The general thought that all world-trouble serves to bring into view the person of Christ, wherever under the preaching of the Gospel that person has been made known. The relation of the world to Him, in its present condition, involves a contradiction. The world has no power in itself to reveal Christ. In the end there must, of course, be harmony between nature and grace, but "the end is not yet." The tendency of the world now is to obscure Christ and to veil Him from our vision. In times of worldly prosperity, in success in business, in the possession of earthly power and fame, it is very difficult to fix the mind on Christ, or to understand Him. So it was with the disciples on the sea. There was no revelation of their Lord's majestic power, in this regard at least, so long as the sea was calm. But when the winds came sweeping down upon them, and they lost control of their vessel, and had no confidence in themselves, and were in extreme distress and instant peril, then He came walking on the waters. At first they had no power to recognize Him, but were filled with terror and alarm. So it is universally with our life. We see not the stars in the sky during the broad light of the day, but only in the darkness of the night; and when the night is the darkest the stars are the brightest. This world we know is indeed empty and vain, but this we do not and somehow cannot truly feel in times of outward prosperity. We need trials in the world to teach us the emptiness and vanity of the world. In this way also we are prepared to look to Christ for help, and at such times He reveals Himself to us by producing that state of mind whereby alone we can apprehend His presence, nearness and power.

II. We see, again, that as the world grows dim to us, our inward vision grows clearer and stronger. In prosperity we do not see the reality and power of the world of grace. But let the world once grow dark to us, and how soon we feel the need of something higher. Then the scales fall from our eyes, and we can see what before was entirely hid from our vision.

This is brought out here in the miracle. In the tempest when all hope had failed, the disciples saw their Master with all the powers of nature under His feet. The first great lesson here is that we learn to apprehend the law that requires this world to disappear that the world beyond may be seen. All hope in this world must be given up before help can come from above and beyond. And the second lesson here is, the relation of Christ to the world, as brought out in this miracle. Not as a common man does He challenge the attention of the disciples, but as being in His own person One who has mastered the world and all its powers. He is in Himself more than the whole world, and His victory is a victory because there was in Him, by virtue of the constitution of His person, a mighty, majestic, conquering power. This is brought out very strikingly in this miracle.

In looking to Him as one who can give us the victory over the world, we have two things for our faith to rest upon. He stands before the disciples in this miracle, first of all, as belonging to the world, and not as having come down upon it, in an outward magical way, from some higher sphere. So He must appear to men generally, in every age, if He would bring them salvation. There is in man a natural shrinking from the forces and powers of a higher, supernatural world. But Christ's presence in the world is not unearthly, for He is a man in all respects as other men, the ideal and perfect man, and as such He belongs to this world. He is a partaker of our human nature. If He were not, there could be no consolation for us in His presence with us. He would be a mere spectre, having no power for our life, and being no object for our faith.

Then, too, on the other hand, He was not of nature but above it. He was not as other men, subject to the powers of the world. As the ideal man having dominion over nature, He shows His disciples in this storm on the sea that the forces and powers of nature were under His feet. He comes to them, not as a spirit, but as their Lord and Master in human form. Not by doctrine can the world be overcome. There is no victory over the world apart from faith in His person. A true faith in Him sees and apprehends the supernatural in the natural. There can be no saving faith in the supernatural merely as such, abstractly and apart from the natural. "It is I," He says: "be not afraid." Faith in the Lord must always unite these two. Aside from such union these can be at best only an empty and barren speculation, and no proper comfort or peace for the human soul, as we see in the fact that so long as the disciples here took Him for a pure spirit they cried out for fear.

III. This miracle, or as we may also truly call it, this parable, exhibits the nature of faith. Faith is not a mere notion or fancy, nor is it a simple acknowledgement of the presence of the spiritual. It has to do with the element of the divine, indeed, but with the divine in organic union with the human. Faith in Christ is faith in the Son of God incarnate. It apprehends Him not only as "conceived by the Holy Ghost," but also as "born of the Virgin Mary." It lays hold on Him as "God manifest in the flesh." Faith needs to be always distinguished from mere intelligence. It is the power of seeing Christ as at work both in the Church and in the world of human history. All that flows forth from His person and work, the Church, the sacraments, mysteries as they all are, are included in the Creed as objects of faith. Faith is something far deeper than mere knowledge. It is not put into men magically, nor conferred upon them in any outward way, but must spring up from one's own nature, mind or spirit, having its roots in our incorporation in the order of grace, whose foundation is in baptism. It cannot grow strong by reasoning, by fancy, or feeling. It must be confronted by the proper objects of faith. These we must keep ever before us: and when they are seen, they can and will excite faith and call out the power of truth. The power lies in the object and comes from it. We see this in the case before us. The disciples were under training. They had never thought of Christ before, neither did it occur to them during the storm to think of Him as walking on the sea. Hence, so long as they regarded Him as an apparition, there was in them a feeling of fear and terror, as believing that they stood in the presence of the purely supernatural. But so soon as they came to see Him as their Master, there was in Him a power of drawing out their faith. They hear His voice, "It is I." The inmost life and power of His being uttering itself in that voice, speaks to the inmost sense of apprehension in them. Peter says, "Lord, if it be thou, bid me come unto thee on the water." That "if" shows that there was at first in his mind a doubt, and some hesitation, yet at the same time a readiness to yield: but his faith grows stronger through the power of the proper object confronting it in the person of the Lord. Hence the deep meaning there is in the creed ever placing anew before us the objects of faith. For faith must ever thus be held close to that which alone can awaken it, and in communion with which alone it can grow. By such communion we are apprehended and taken up by these objects into their own lofty and exalted spiritual sphere. We do not rise, we cannot rise of ourselves. So Christ appeared to His disciples on the sea as standing on a higher plane, one to which they had to rise. The lower sphere does not and cannot of itself rise to the higher: the higher alone has power to reach down, lay hold of and lift up the lower to its own exalted place.

For Peter there was a venture here, but not a blind one. He could not fortify himself by his own reason, in thus desiring to go down on the water. So must the sinner boldly venture himself on Christ. And behold the grandeur of the spectacle—a sinful man furnished with power to walk on the water, giving thus an exhibition of the power over nature which was conferred on man in his original creation. He threw himself off from the natural knowledge he had, into the waters where he had nothing but the word of Christ. In such a sublime act as this, the soul passes from time to eternity. Faith is secure only so long as it is firm, steady, continually looking and clinging to Christ. This is the one only condition of its security. So soon as this ceases, faith is gone. Peter saw the winds boisterous and the waves tossing: he looked away from Christ to the elements around him, and began to sink, and cried out for help, "Lord, save me!"

This great miracle has a meaning as well for us as for the disciples. We are now in the world, whose symbol is the tossing, heaving, restless sea. We are in a frail bark at the mercy of the powers of the world which we of ourselves and in our own strength are helpless to resist or to overcome.

But—we are surrounded by another order of existence, so near to us, so present with us, that if our vision were clear, and our eyes were not holden, we should see Christ before us every moment. His voice sounds out to us across this great, tempest-tossed world-sea, as it did to the disciples of old, "It is I: be not afraid!" We need to set the great objects of faith constantly before us at all times and make them also objects of our most prayerful regard. They are within our reach, and presently at hand—let us ever hold ourselves toward them in the attitude of faith.

———, *1869*.

The Fourth Sunday after The Epiphany.

THE PRECIOUSNESS OF FAITH.

The Second Epistle General of St. Peter i. 1.

"*Simon Peter, a servant and an apostle of Jesus Christ, to them that have obtained like precious faith with us through the righteousness of God and our Saviour Jesus Christ.*"

In the Epistle to the Hebrews faith is defined as "The substance of things hoped for, the evidence of things not seen." And St. Paul says, "We look not at the things which are seen, but at the things which are not seen: for the things which are seen are temporal, but the things which are not seen are eternal." Faith is the power of looking beyond the world of sense and time to the world that is invisible and eternal.

This power, however, is not to be confounded with poetic fancy, by the exercise of which it is also possible, in a certain sense, to pass beyond the range of ordinary life and to communicate with things unseen and eternal. Faith differs from this in that it is an actual apprehension of the eternal and unseen as being presently at hand, the very "substance of things hoped for." Such a power as this can be exercised only when the objects themselves are felt to be at hand in their own proper nature. Faith is felt, in the very beginning of it, to have direct reference to these objects, and can have no existence at all apart from them. By the objects of faith we are to understand, in a word, divine revelation. Divine revelation is one, though it may be considered as being made up of many different parts or factors, and faith may be regarded as being exercised toward these different parts. In this way the faith of the Old Testament saints is one with the faith of the New Testament saints. The ultimate object of faith is the New Testament revelation—the Word of God revealed in full in the person of Christ. Faith, in its full evangelical sense, is strictly conditioned by this object. It cannot exist without it, just as the eye cannot exist without the light by which its activity is conditioned. Faith is exercised in the element of this invisible world of revelation, and depends on the presence of the object itself under which the revelation becomes complete. "This is the work of God, that ye believe on him whom he hath sent." "This is eternal life that they might know thee, the only true God, and Jesus Christ whom thou hast sent." There is no room even to conceive of faith apart from the person of Christ. This is the kind of faith we find in the Apostles' Creed, and in all the ancient creeds. The exercise of faith that is called for in the Creed is not 'theological reflection, but is an activity of mind on the part of the believer which lays hold of this great object, Christ, from whom all the articles of the Creed flow forth. Our belief in Christ, as expressed in the Apostles' Creed, is based upon this self-authenticating power. Just as objects in the natural world impress themselves upon us by their own presence, through the medium of light, so is it here.

Under this view, faith is seen to be something truly great. For, how does it come? St. Peter addresses his epistle "To them that have obtained like precious faith with us through the righteousness of God and our Saviour Jesus Christ." According to what has just now been said, faith is an activity of the human mind or spirit; just as much so as is imagination or intelligence. It does not belong to, cannot be conferred upon a man in an outward way, and is not to be regarded as anything magical. There must be a necessity and ground for it in the original constitution of the soul itself; otherwise we could not at all attain to it. " There is a spirit in man, and the inspiration of the Almighty giveth them understanding." The ground of faith, as an activity of the mind or spirit, rests in the original constitution of man. There is an affinity of our spirits with the Divine Spirit, and with the invisible world; there is a power in us by which the soul of man reaches out beyond time and sense to things that are spiritual and eternal. This is an original prerogative of our nature. Yet, at the same time the exercise of this power depends on the presence and influence of the Spirit of God. Revelation does not create faith, nor insert it into the soul as if it had not been there before. It is in the mind constitutionally as a possibility. As is said in the passage above quoted from the book of Job, " There is a spirit in man;" but it is also added, " and the inspiration of the Almighty giveth them understanding." The Holy Spirit must and does work on the minds of men; He broods over them, as on creation's morn He "moved upon the face of the waters," bringing order out of chaos, and unfolding the possibilities of the human spirit. In this way this original possibility of faith becomes, under the operation of the Holy Ghost, the power of looking at "things that are not seen and eternal."

So much, then, is involved in the Apostle's words, "To them that have obtained like precious faith" through God and Christ. To them the divine lot has fallen to have this capacity for apprehending heavenly realities brought forth and developed by being operated upon from above and beyond. In the text it is worthy of being observed that faith is not regarded as something self-produced, but as depending continually on the operation of the Holy Spirit.

Furthermore, this faith is set before us as something exceedingly " precious," valuable. It deserves to be considered in an eminent degree. " To them that have obtained like precious faith." What else is there in all the world so truly precious as faith? There is nothing of such vital and fundamental account. Its character of preciousness suggests its rarity and difficulty of attainment, for these are the peculiar characteristics of that which is precious universally. Faith is something rare, although it has its ground and possibility in every human soul. Nor is it hard to understand how or why the attainment of faith is something difficult; for although it is one of the deepest powers or principles of the mind, yet it has been overlaid or held in bondage by a more superficial nature which has to do directly with the material world—with things that are seen and temporal—and all this, as we know, by reason of the fall of man from that state in which he was originally created. The things of this world so take the attention and so absorb the interest of the soul, that this deeper power of apprehending higher things is prevented from being exercised, the natural crowding out the spiritual, and the temporal allowing no room for the eternal. The world of nature and sense, by which we are made to fall a prey to natural appetites, stands fearfully in the way of deeper instincts. It is a weight by which our minds are dragged down to the earth—a force bending and binding us to the vanities of the world.

In this respect faith is something rare. The great majority of men are occupied almost exclusively with the world of sense, and if their attention is directed to anything higher, it is only in the way of thought. But it is not enough to communicate with a higher world only in the way of thought. Such a communication is, after all, only by fancy; and it is because of the universal tendency in this direction that faith is hard to produce, and difficult to maintain. When St. Paul says of himself that he looked not on things seen and temporal but on things unseen and eternal, he unconsciously presents in his own person one of the most sublime spectacles on which it is possible for us to fix our gaze. A man that is in the world, and is surrounded by the things of the world, and yet has power to look beyond all, to things unseen and eternal, presents the highest exhibition of human virtue.

Faith is difficult not only in the way we have mentioned, but also and furthermore from the faithless atmosphere prevailing in the world. There is a lack of incentive to its exercise in our entire surroundings. If society were universally governed by christian principle, it would not seem so hard for men to exercise faith. But the very opposite of this is the case. The world of morality by which men are commonly governed is led away captive by the presence and power of material things. This is the case in art, science, culture; the whole social and political world revolves in the orbit of that which is seen and temporal. Of themselves, and by their own power, none of these ever get beyond this narrow scope, nor ever rise to the apprehension of a higher life. In the exercise of faith, then, what disadvantages are we not called upon to sustain! We are challenged to keep in exercise that faculty or power of the soul which the whole world around us is calculated to deaden, if not indeed to destroy. In these circumstances faith is necessarily difficult. It is the property of only a few. And even amongst those who profess Christ there are still only comparatively few who do possess it in its proper fulness and power. It was with reference to this downward tendency of the human spirit that our Saviour said, "When the Son of Man cometh, shall he find faith on the earth?" When, in His glorious second advent, He shall break in upon the present order of things, and come forth suddenly presented to the minds of men, shall He find any reasonable number of them in the possession of this mighty power of faith? Well may the Apostle congratulate those to whom this epistle was written, in the language of the text!

The preciousness of faith appears when we consider its intrinsic value. If it were possessed by all men, it would lose none of its great value. We need not dwell at length on this point. As soon as we come to see what faith obtains for us, and what a power it is in the soul of man, we need no further argument to convince us of its importance. How much there is, at many places, in God's word exhorting to its exercise and descriptive of its exceeding excellence. Even in the Old Testament we find much of this, as in the book of Proverbs, for example, where the writer dwells at length and frequently upon the blessedness of wisdom—words which may well be applied to faith; for the faith of the New Testament is, in meaning, synonymous with the wisdom of the Old—"Happy is the man that findeth wisdom, and the man that getteth understanding. For the merchandise of it is better than the merchandise of silver, and the gain thereof than fine gold. She is more precious than rubies, and all the things that thou canst desire are not to be compared unto her. Length of days is in her right hand; and in her left hand riches and honor. Her ways are ways of pleasantness, and all her paths are peace."

It would be easy to show that faith is the highest form of intelligence. When once compared with this power of the soul, all other activities whatsoever are seen to be poor, mean and weak. What illumination of the mind, for instance, may for a single moment be compared with that high enlightenment which comes through that faith by which we see light in God's light? If, in this way, "thine eye be single, thy whole body shall be full of light: but if thine eye be evil, thy whole body shall be full of darkness. If, therefore, the light that is in thee be darkness, how great is that darkness!" If we look at the case properly, we shall see that the most strenuous exercise of thought is as nothing when compared with the illumination of faith. Without that, there is but little difference between the philosopher and the fool. In truth, the highest kind of spiritual activity is that which is involved in the act of faith. Faith enlarges the mind far beyond any other kind of knowledge or science. It involves a wide freedom to which the spirit of man cannot be introduced in any other way. It arms the very life of a man with the strongest weapons, and inspires him with the most invincible courage. Should we compare all physical and intellectual powers with the power of faith, we should find that while the former plant themselves, as it were, on a created fulcrum, the latter rests upon the living God.

Faith grounds itself in God. The subject comes to have part in His Kingdom. Faith is the power of miracles, in the Old Testament and in the New. The power of faith is expressed by St. John where he says, " This is the victory that overcometh the world, even our faith." It is a power that exceeds all other powers in the world. And the very essence of man's dignity consists in his having the world under him. All acquisition of wealth and power, what is it, but an evidence that men instinctively are seeking for the mastery of the world, blindly feeling after this mighty power of faith. They cannot help themselves—they are instinctively driven to it. This is the problem with which the world in its fallen state is wrestling. The Apostle says, "This is the victory that overcometh the world, even our faith"—that is, faith in the person of Christ, and in nothing else; because in Him alone the powers of the world are overcome.

"Who is he that overcometh the world?" This is a question which challenges all for an answer, the philosopher, the politician, the men of natural science, and of all the arts. Who is he? It is none other than "He that believeth that Jesus is the Son of God." Nothing more than this is needed to bring home the significance of the congratulation contained in the text. Sir Humphrey Davy, a most distinguished man of Science, at the close of his life, said, "I envy no man the gift of beauty, honor or power: but if there be one thing I value above all else, it is the gift of faith." This is the testimony of a man most learned in his department.

Is this power in us? If it is, then we should neglect no opportunity for the cultivation and development of it. It is indeed the gift of God, in the sense that it is possible only in view of what God has done and has given in the Gospel. The development of this principle or power depends upon the presence of the object with which it is employed. This is so not only with faith—it is the same with all our faculties and powers. The eye cannot be strengthened without the presence of the light. All the bodily senses are awakened, developed, strengthened only by the objects with which they are intended to deal. Such is the relation between the inward and the outward everywhere in our lives. And this law holds good pre-eminently in our relation to the world that is unseen and eternal. If we think not of "those things that are above, where Christ sitteth on the right hand of God;" if we do not keep them in mind, if we have not at all to do with them, but are led away continually by the things of this transitory and perishable world, how can this power of faith, so pricelessly precious as we have seen it to be, ever arise in our souls, how can it ever grow strong and great? We can require our minds to look at these things; these things are at hand for us, being brought nigh to us in the Gospel: we have power to come under their gracious influence. Setting before ourselves Jesus Christ, meditating upon Him, His character and mighty works, we shall be excited to faith, and faith will thereby be established in our souls. So the Apostle exhorts us, " Let us lay aside every weight, and the sin which doth so easily beset us, and let us run with patience the race that is set before us"———But this exertion on our part, this exercise of our own subjective powers is not by itself sufficient. There must be something more. Hence the Apostle goes on immediately to add,"——"looking unto Jesus, the author and finisher of our faith, who for the joy that was set before him endured the cross, despising the shame, and is set down at the right hand of the throne of God. For consider him who endured such contradiction of sinners against himself, lest ye be wearied and faint in your minds. Ye have not yet re-sisted unto blood, striving against sin."

January 30, 1870.

The Sixth Sunday after The Epiphany.

JESUS THE ONLY MEDIATOR.

John i. 51.

"*And He saith unto them, Verily, verily I say unto you, Hereafter ye shall see heaven open, and the angels of God ascending and descending on the Son of Man.*"

THIS text occurs in connection with the call of Philip and Nathanael. Nathanael having expressed surprise at our Saviour's most intimate knowledge of him, our Saviour replied, " Because I said unto thee, I saw thee under the fig tree, believest thou? Thou shalt see greater things than these." Then follows the text.

There is here an allusion undoubtedly to the vision which occurred to Jacob at Bethel, on his way to Padan-Aram, when he beheld the ladder set up on the earth, the top of it reaching to heaven, and the angels of God ascending and descending on it; which was undoubtedly a symbol and pledge of that communication between earth and heaven which God was pleased to establish in the way of grace, beginning with the promises in patriarchal times, and being finally completed in the Incarnation; " Hereafter ye shall see heaven open, and the angels of God ascending and descending on the Son of Man."

These words, of course, imply that outside of this communion of grace, there always is and must be a chasm between God and man; a chasm which cannot be bridged over in any other way, being the result of sin, by which man is estranged from God. By reason of sin, God is turned away from man, His love turning into wrath. This fact of estrangement between the two is certified and made known not simply by the testimony of God's revelation to men, but also by the universal experience of men themselves, who everywhere and in every age instinctively feel and know that they are not in right relation to God. Whether men are conscious of it or not, the great problem of humanity has always been the bridging over of this deep, dark, and awful chasm of separation, in order to secure not only the hope of immortality, but also a present sense of peace. In all ages of the world men have endeavored to solve this problem. These endeavors have been all in vain. No man, philosopher, statesman or poet, has ever been able to bridge this chasm over. For it affects the whole world of nature, which in its own measure has suffered from the fall; and as nature finds its completion in man, there can be no separation between man and God, that does not also involve, or draw along with it, a separation between the natural and the supernatural worlds. The supernatural world—that world in which God dwells, and in which alone the true happiness of men can be found—from this we are so separated that by no human power whatever can we again attain to it. And yet, created life cannot be full and free, cannot at all attain to its proper end and aim without standing in direct communication with "the Father of lights, with whom is neither variableness nor shadow of turning."

The one great question for the world, then, is the solution to the problem of the relation between God and man, the bridging over of this chasm, the constituting of a proper living communion and fellowship between our spirits and the Father of spirits. So long as our nature is in this respect unsatisfied, we can find no rest or peace. And in view of this it is that our Saviour says, "Hereafter ye shall see heaven open, and the angels of God ascending and descending on the Son of Man,"—that is to say, during my ministry in the world, and in the history of the Church. "The angels of God" here represent the idea of full communication—"angels ascending" that is, bearing upward to God the thoughts, feelings, prayers of men: "Angels descending," that is, bringing down to men the rewards of righteousness in the way of spiritual illumination, of spiritual power to overcome the world, and to gain the victory over our present fallen state. All this is to be brought to pass through the ministry of the angels. We cannot at all explain that ministry. It is enough to know that it has an accredited place in the economy of salvation. The writer of the Epistle to the Hebrews, speaks of the ministry of the angels; in the first chapter of that Epistle, and particularly in the last verse, where he says, "Are they not all ministering spirits, sent forth to minister for them who shall be heirs of salvation?" And our Saviour here says, "Hereafter ye shall see the angels of God"—not so much with the outward eye, although the seeing of the angels did even extend to that, when Christ was in the flesh; but more especially "ye shall see" with the inward eye of the spirit, by an apprehension of faith. In this way pre-eminently men were to see and know that the way of communication between heaven and earth was for them open, through the Son of Man.

Here it is most important to observe that this whole new order of grace, thus established, was and is still confined to the person of the Son of Man. This title, "The Son of Man," is made much of by our Saviour, and has a special and a most profound significance. He is "The Son of God," indeed, and yet also and at the same time "The Son of Man"; and it is in virtue of this latter close relationship to our humanity that our salvation is rendered possible. He was a man like unto us: bone of our bone, flesh of our flesh; "conceived by the Holy Ghost, born of the Virgin Mary." This title, "The Son of Man," is a designation conveying a deep meaning. It involves the conception of a central, fundamental relation to our human life, such as belongs to no other man, not even to the greatest hero in all the world, but only to The Man, Jesus of Nazareth. Our Saviour always had a striking and mysterious way of assuming to Himself this central position, and of claiming the full force and significance of it. All other persons He claimed must surround Him, in the way of faith, and love, and truth. This central position of Christ reaches further and deeper even than did the analogous relation in which Adam stood. Christ is "The Son of Man," and as such He is "the first-born of every creature," in a most profound sense, as He is also "the first-born from the dead." He is the source of life and immortality, brought to pass by a struggle with sin, death and hell.

It is in this light that His relation to humanity comes fairly into view, and His title, "The Son of Man," is seen to be full of meaning. "Ye shall see the angels of God ascending and descending"—not on others or on the life of the race at large. This latter is the view taken by many; it is the favorite interpretation put upon this text by humanitarianism in every age, the supposition being that a communication had now been opened up between heaven and the whole human family in a general way. Neither did the angels of God descend on the philosophers and heroes in ancient times, nor will they do so now. Though vast and glorious is their work, it is yet not on them that the angels descend. There is a sense indeed in which the heroes of the world may be said to resemble Christ, namely in respect of that central position which He occupied relatively to the family of man. This central position, occupied by certain great and representative men in various stages of history, is the result of the operation of a universal law, according to which men cannot find their true completion in themselves in a solitary or isolated way, but are constitutionally constrained to seek their completion in clustering around certain central personalities. Such central persons comprehend in themselves a life wider than their own; they are caught up, as it were, into a higher sphere. We see that law exemplified everywhere, the circles of personal complementation becoming wider and wider in the onflowing stream of our human life. In the large circles, the central persons are the great heroes of our humanity in the world of science, politics, philanthropy, etc.

Now, there is an analogy between the position occupied by such persons and that grand central position which only Christ fills in reference to the entire family of man. And this brings into view the fact that the quickening power of humanity which they radiate, comes not from below but from above. Central men assume this position not as the result of thought and reflection, and deliberation on their part, but because they constitutionally gather up into themselves the sense and meaning of other lives, and actualize it. And when such men do actualize the otherwise inexpressible significance of other lives of which they are the representatives, there is such a force brought to bear upon them from beyond themselves, as that it is a kind of inspiration from the very bosom of eternity. They become inspired; in a deep sense of the word they are prophets.

This is true of all who become truly great among men. It is true of every revelation of the truth. But in every case the force, the power which utters itself in and through such representative men, does not come from the multitude, but through the representative personality *from beyond*. This is an interesting analogy, forasmuch as it beautifully illustrates the entire naturalness of our Saviour's central position in the circle of our humanity as "the Son of Man."

To return, however, to the point in question, we say that in the history of the past ages we do not find the highest powers of humanity—powers on which the redemption of the world depends—powers which come from heaven—we do not, I say, find these powers descending on any except on Christ. Important as men in their several spheres may be, they have yet no redeeming power. Just now, more than any other time, art, science, politics are in danger of losing sight of the true character of the Gospel by reducing it to a mere humanitarian agency. But Christ says, "Ye shall see heaven open, and the angels of God ascending and descending"—where? "On the Son of Man!" and nowhere else. One man is capable of representing some particular form of our life, but Christ was a leader and a representative, not only of one age, but of all ages. It is not possible that any hero—even the very greatest—whose inspiration is of necessity partial and relative, can be the medium of full and absolute communion with the spiritual world. In order that any one may have such a position, divinity must be joined to humanity. Such a person must indeed be " conceived by the Holy Ghost and born of the Virgin Mary."

This we have in our Saviour, Jesus Christ, who is both the Son of God and the Son of Man. " Hereafter ye shall see heaven open, and the angels of God ascending and descending on the Son of Man." How all this is to be brought to pass it is not necessary now to set forth, for this would carry us through the whole range of the gospel. But we can see, now, that our Saviour's person, being such as to unite the human and the divine natures, the chasm between God and Man, of which we have been speaking, is now in Him bridged over, and only in Him. Only here have we the root and ground of our redemption. " Hereafter ye shall see heaven open "—the disciples saw this during the time of His earthly ministry—saw it in all the works which constitute His continual Epiphany—saw it in His baptism, when the Holy Ghost descended on Him in the form of a dove—saw it, in brief, from this time forward to the time of His crucifixion. His miracles were wrought before them. It is true, miracles were wrought in the Old Testament by the power of God, but they evidently had reference to the miracles wrought by Christ. Christ Himself may be said to be the great miracle of all miracles. We cannot at all believe in the New Testament miracles with a true christian faith, except as that faith is conditioned upon a living faith in Christ Himself. No number of miracles could have been sufficient to authenticate the divine mission of our Saviour, apart from His own person. These miracles were so many verifications of His divinity, and of the descent of the angels of God on the Son of Man. " Hereafter ye shall see the angels of God descending," was the promise of the Saviour at the opening of His ministry; and they did see it. They saw it in the water made wine, they saw it in the healing of the lepers and of the nobleman's son, they saw it in the power displayed by Him in walking on the sea, and in calling the dead to life; and those who were with Him on that occasion saw it pre-eminently in His transfiguration. These were only glimpses, however, of the power and majesty which abode continually in His person. Thus were the angels of God ascending and descending on Him, and this fact His followers could not help but see and feel when they were brought near to Him in spirit. They saw it in His words as well as in His works, and were persuaded that "never man spake like this man;" and that His words were the "words of eternal life." And especially were they convinced of it by His resurrection and ascension, and by the descent of the Holy Ghost, who came upon them with even outward signs and wonders.

And this has been the experience of christians in all ages since. Christ alone has power to bring us into communion with the higher world. The christian system thus possesses a power far beyond any dreamed of by the pagan world, in solving the great problem or riddle of our humanity. Did time permit, we might show how all true illumination for the world must come in the way indicated in the text. The light of the nineteenth century, of which so much is said nowaday, how poor and mean it is, after all, when set over against that great flood of light which comes from the gospel of our Saviour! By Him alone is the chasm bridged over. "There is none other name under heaven given among men whereby we must be saved."

Here, in conclusion, I wish to commend to your constant consideration the thought that this is the highest end of existence. Here there is offered for your acceptance a power over sin, both on the theoretical side of the reason, and also on the practical side of the will. The completion of our being must be brought about by a power strictly supernatural. The great and alarming danger of our age is humanitarianism—a seeking after the completion of our life and the removal of the evils which afflict the world, to be brought about by the operation of laws, forces, powers, agencies resident in humanity as such. The pleasing dream of men's souls now is that society is to be born again—not from above, but from beneath—not by the grace of the gospel, but by the illumination of science and art. But if these powers of man be trusted instead of the power of the gospel, to bridge over the wide gulf between God and man, they will invariably be found a mere spider's web. The ruin is far too wide and deep to be reached in any such way.

If there be one truth perfectly clear, it is that salvation comes from above, and that in the most fully supernatural manner. Why else did the Word become incarnate? or why does Christ so frequently, over and over again, proclaim Himself the source of life? Why does He say, "No man knoweth the Father save the Son," and again, "No man hath ascended up to heaven but he that came down from heaven, even the Son of man which is in heaven?" This is the great problem with which heathen mythology wrestled, as we see in the story of Hercules, for instance, in which case the struggle was more in the way of an outward conflict, whereas in the case of others in the heathen mythology it was more inward and spiritual.

In reference to this the Saviour says—not merely, of course, in reference to the heathen prophets and law-givers, but to those of the Old Testament as well—" No man hath ascended up into heaven:" no man can ascend; no man shall hereafter ascend. No philosopher or poet has ever in this way climbed the heavens. " No man hath ascended up into heaven!" This is one of the grandest declarations of the whole Gospel. " No man hath ascended up to heaven, but he that came down from heaven, even the Son of man"—not the Son of God —" which is in heaven." In this capacity He was glorified as the highest hero of our humanity, and in this character He commends Himself to our faith, even as He challenged the faith of His disciples of old. And it is in this sublime character, also, that He is commended to us, as He was to them, by "the voice from the excellent glory" in His transfiguration on the mountain, and by the same voice at His baptism in the Jordan, " This is my beloved Son in whom I am well pleased; hear ye Him."

February 6, 1870.

The Sunday before Lent—Quinquagesima.

THE LAW OF SPIRITUAL VISION.

Matthew vi. 22-23.

" The light of the body is the eye: if therefore thine eye be single, thy whole body shall be full of light. But if thine eye be evil, thy whole body shall be full of darkness. If therefore the light that is in thee be darkness, how great is that darkness!"

WE have here a familiar image to represent a great moral truth. The act of sight involves two sides of existence which reciprocally condition each other. First: it cannot take place without the presence of light, and this is of an objective character. But, secondly, the act of seeing depends on what is comprehended in the constitution of our own person; that is, it is conditioned by the eye. Were there no light there could, of course, be no sight; but, were there no eye, there could be no sight either. Without an eye wherewith to see, there can be no vision, no matter how much light may be at hand. If there be no eye, all light, however brilliant, is only darkness.

The relation between the eye and the light is not such that the eye becomes a mere passive agent for taking in the light. The eye could not at all apprehend or take in the light if there were not in it a character corresponding to the constitution of the light. The eye is in itself luminiferous, or, (if I may use the word) phosphorescent —that is to say, light-bearing, for the purposes of vision. We know that light may be produced by the eye itself. When it is struck it emits light to itself. On closing the eye, after beholding some brilliant object, the eye of itself reproduces the light and the image of the object.

There is too in light itself, considered as something objective, a corresponding pre-adaptation to the constitution of the eye. The meeting and mutual complementation of these two activities, the one objective the other subjective, is what we call vision, or sight. It is no doubt in view of, and with a perfect understanding of this relation, that our Saviour says, "The light of the body"—of the whole person, that is—"is the eye." The light of the body is not the element at large which touches all the members of the body, but there is one organ, or member, which is the medium of its communication to the entire body, namely, the eye. Through this organ it exerts its power and influence over the entire organism. In this way, light being mediated to the body by the eye, men may know the things around them, how to walk, how to work and act. Here, of course, the light is the condition, and all depends on the character of that member of the body which is the organ for its apprehension and communication. "The light of the body is the eye—if, therefore, thine eye be single"—that is, answerable to the light; if it have a light-bearing, a light-representing capacity and power, then "the whole body is full of light." "But if thine eye be evil"—if it lack the power to respond to the outward element of the light; if there be no correspondence between the two, no power in the eye to receive, to mediate and interpret the light for the body as a whole—"thy whole body shall be full of darkness. If therefore the light that is in thee be darkness, how great is that darkness!" For this state of things there is, of course, no remedy.

The goodness of the eye depends on its simplicity, or singleness. Only then will it well perform the high functions of its office. The eye that sees things in a confused way is not thus single, whole, sound, efficient for the purposes of the organism, and will mediate darknesss instead of light.

This is a simple and yet at the same time a very striking image of a profound moral truth. There is a correspondence between the world of nature and the world of mind which renders such an image or figure most profoundly forcible. The correspondence is not accidental or simply external, but involves or is based upon an inward, constitutional relationship, and by virtue of such relationship things physical stand for and are commonly taken as symbols of things ethical and spiritual. Thus light stands for truth, and darkness for error. The relation between the two is not merely fanciful or conventional, as if this taking of natural things to represent moral truths were the result of arbitrary agreement. It rests upon something far deeper than that—upon an inner, organic, constitutional relationship. It is easy to see that there is an inner relation between seeing and thinking, for instance. All thinking begins in seeing; in taking in the outward light and the images of outward objects in a way far different from that in which an animal, for example, sees them, or takes them in; for a man sees, not passively, but with the power of intellectual perception. We can see, in this way, how the exercise of this faculty of sight rises to the highest possible conception of the human reason. Seeing and thinking are closely related, as are also light and truth.

The question arises, wherein consists the seeing of the mind? To this different answers may be given. There may be a lower or a higher seeing. You may say the eye of the soul begins to be exercised in intellectual perception, when by sensation the mind receives impressions from abroad and mentally reacts upon them, and in this way acquires knowledge of them. This is something quite different from what is possible, in the act of seeing, to the animal nature. Animals do not look at objects as men do. In the human world seeing involves an intellectual as well as a physical act. The higher vision comes in through the medium of the lower. The apprehension on the part of the human spirit is not only a natural vision. It is more inward than this, involving intelligence, and is something truly great, challenging our admiration when we compare it with sight as exercised by the lower orders of existence where conscious mind, or reason, does not exist; and it would seem to some that this great power of intelligent apprehension is so great and high a power that by the pure and unaided exercise thereof man may hope to solve the problem of his existence; and when such persons read this passage —"The light of the body is the eye"—they imagine that the reference is entirely to something intellectual and rational; that it means that if your reason and intelligence are well developed, sound and whole, your whole being shall be full of light. There is, of course, much truth in this view; but taken separately and by itself, it does not give us the full sense of the text.

There is a sense in which the text applies in full, and that is when we are in proper sympathy with our Saviour. There are some who consider the single eye to mean conscience. If that be pure and single and sound, they say, then the whole body shall be full of light. This comes nearer to the truth, but still does not bring it wholly into view. The full force and sense of the text we apprehend as coming into view only when we rise to the highest stage of intelligence in man, which we do not find in the reason, purely as such, but in the will. In the reason we have a power which produces science; but there is a higher power in man than even the reason, high indeed as that is—the will, which is the other side of our spiritual nature. We have the theoretical reason, the power of intelligence, the object of which is truth, science. Then we have the practical reason, the power of action—a power which is not merely able to follow out a course of action set before it, but a power of originating its own determination for itself. It is the same reason both in the will and the understanding, of course, but in the understanding reason manifests itself in one way, in the will in another way.

Now, this is what we are to understand by "The light of the body is the eye"—the highest sense of man's life as this makes itself felt in the depths of his own moral being, and causes him to regard one end only as the true end of existence. To such a "single eye" all other ends and purposes must take a subordinate position. The understanding can propose an end, and set it before the will, and the will may follow it as supreme and controlling. This end may be wealth, power, or some high, ambitious purpose; but sooner or later such an end is found not to be the true end of existence, and there is then a want of singleness in the eye; it sees double; its images are misty and cloudy. The proposed end may be something high, glorious and great, yet if it be not that end which the nature of the will requires, it is not possible that the eye should be single. There is a sense of something wrong, something wanting for the proper completion of the existence. Only when the object proposed is in full harmony with the will of the Saviour can we have that singleness of the eye spoken of in the text.

In all seeing, whether physical or intellectual, the importance of the objective element must not be overlooked. In the constitution of the human will it is necessary to know where the proper end of existence lies, as something objective and external first of all. This great end and purpose of life (upon which we cannot now dwell at length) is set before us, in a word, in the incarnation of our Lord, and is the only proper object of our faith. It is evident that there can be no faith, which is the same as seeing—the two are really one and the same—no singleness of the eye, except by the presence of the Truth, as an objective power or element, acting upon us from without in the form of God's revelation. We cannot project our own notions of truth, as it were, out into an intellectual space, and then make them the objects of our vision or apprehension. The Truth must be at hand, not in the way of fancy or imagination or speculation, but actually present, as being the very presence of the Incarnate Word. "This is the work of God," says Christ, not that you believe in the creations of your own fancy or reason, but that you believe in the great fact and mystery of the incarnation. There is no faith in theological speculation. There is none in any department of our intellectual life, except as the eye is directed to Jesus Christ. There is no growing in grace where experimental religion, as it is called, rests upon its own ever-varying states and frames of mind. Experimental religion, to be of the right kind, must be an abiding, constant communication with objective grace.

So much is included in the text—"If thine eye be single, thy whole body shall be full of light." How could it be otherwise? "But, if the light that is in thee be darkness, how great is that darkness!" We can here at once see, according to this profound law of spiritual seeing, as laid down by our Saviour, what is the general cause of unbelief, wherever an honest infidelity exists. Such men are not able to satisfy themselves even of the truth of Christianity. The position of the infidel is a false position. What is his position? Why, he affects to stand quite outside and independent of the whole world of grace—apart from Christ and Christianity—and seeks by an intellectual analysis to make them intelligible to himself. He will not place himself in position to allow these to authenticate themselves to him, and seeks to prove the higher truth by the lower. Because he cannot prove the sun by looking away from the sun, he denies that there is a sun. And yet he feels that he is an honest infidel! Verily, he is to be pitied!

All truth, and especially all truth that is fundamental, must enter into a man in a practical way, or on the practical side, on the side of the practical reason—the will—rather than on the side of the pure reason—the understanding. To prove such a truth without experiencing and practicing it, is a contradiction, an impossibility. And yet that is the position of the infidel. Such a person needs to see that the highest form of our rational being is in the will, on the practical side, and not at all on the theoretical. The first and chief end of our being is that the will, not the understanding primarily, but the will, must be brought into harmony with the truth. Such is the relation between the objective and the subjective sides here, that the will never can be true to its own nature and constitution without apprehending and sanctioning the highest form of all existence as we are confronted by it in the person of Jesus Christ.

"If any man will do His will"—*is willing* to do His will—"he shall know of the doctrine." Two acts are involved here: first, the will to do, and secondly the doing. The two cannot be so separated as to have the one without the other. Furthermore, the knowing of the doctrine depends on the doing of His will. It is not possible that the knowledge of the Spirit can be reached in any other way. This shows infidelity to be unscientific and unphilosophical at once. The only way by which the faith can be established is by holding our will in full harmony with the divine will. This constitutes "the single eye"—the simplicity, wholeness, soundness of the will in its relation to the truth. By the exercise and use of this we have an unerring assurance of faith, and possess that singleness of the eye whereby our whole being, body, soul and spirit, shall be full of light.

February 27, 1870.

The Third Sunday in Lent.

HELP FROM ABOVE.

Psalm 130, v. 1.

"*Out of the depths have I cried unto thee, O Lord.*"

It is from these words of the Psalmist that the language of the collect for this day is taken, while at the same time they furnish the key-note for the proper understanding of both the Gospel and the Epistle Lesson. The collect reads thus—

"*Almighty God, who hast been the hope and confidence of Thy people in all ages; mercifully regard, we beseech Thee, the prayer with which we cry unto Thee out of the depths, and stretch forth the right hand of Thy majesty for our salvation and defense, through Jesus Christ Our Lord. Amen.*"

The idea here expressed by the words "the depths," is that of great trial and sorrow. This may indeed be under a purely physical aspect, as in the suffering of pain in sickness or otherwise, but the moral and spiritual element is chief. We feel that all pain is but the expression of moral misery. So that in the language, "Out of the depths," there is a plain reference to the common misery of our life superinduced by sin.

There are in the image itself, here presented for our consideration, three conceptions—

I. That of a fall. II. That of a feeling of despair—a feeling that the fall leaves us in a position whence we cannot escape by our own unaided powers, but that we are under the absolute necessity of looking up to powers above and beyond for help and deliverance. And III., The idea of deliverance from above; deliverance not from the depths, but from a plane above and beyond them. These three conceptions enter into any moral pain into which men fall, but they have their full and proper signification only in view of man's spiritual fall. Under this view, the text forms the key-note of the lessons for the day, and is a fine expression of the general spirit of the Lenten season considered as a whole. As we saw last sunday, these lessons bring out the conflict between Christ and the world, beginning in the temptation and ending in the victory on the cross. On the previous sunday we saw the conflict of Christ with the kingdom of evil in the form of a single example: but in both the Scripture lessons and in the collect for this day we are referred to a conflict with the powers of evil under a wider and more general view. The whole world, especially as culminating in humanity, is here regarded as lying in sin. The state in which the world is universally is not its ideal or original state. The whole world is fallen. Even the external world of nature may be regarded in one view as a falling away from the world of spirit. It is remote from God. It is only a shadow of the spiritual. The relation between the natural and the spiritual is such that we all feel that the natural depends on the spiritual. The more we look at the relation, and reflect upon it, the more clearly do we see that the natural is but a dark and shadowy reflection of the spiritual. Thus, time is only a shadow of eternity, and space a shadow of heaven. Heaven is not a mere continuation of our space existence. So also our whole time-life is a falling away from our higher, complete life

—and it would be so even had man not fallen. Were we not hindered by sin, we should feel and realize this more; we should see that our life here is only a parable of that higher life: that this is not our home; that here we cannot rest, nor find our satisfaction. Were our eyes not blinded thus by sin, we should see with infinitely greater clearness than we are now capable of, that the end of our being cannot be found in this world, that here we cannot rest.

This being the general relation between heaven and earth in its normal character, we are prepared to see that our whole human life has fallen away from sublime heights, and is now lying helpless in the depths. That we are thus fallen from a nobler state we feel in our inmost consciousness. We have within us the feeling of something higher—a reminiscence, as some think, of a higher condition of the soul in a pre-existent state. But be that as it may, sin is plainly, and in the very conception of it, a lapse from a higher element of existence to a lower. The existence of man is no longer held in proper connection with its ultimate ground. It has somehow experienced a fall, or lapse—as if an existence in the air, like that of a bird, should sink down out of its own native and necessary element, and be doomed to the earth, or sink into a still lower order in the water. Thus we conceive our present condition to be one of a lapse or fall from a higher element to a lower.

We cannot at all account for such a lapse or fall. It antedates our exprience. We cannot get behind it, or reach above or beyond it in any way, so as to understand even the possibility of it. "Sin entered into the world" —but how it did so we cannot explain. If we could understand it, it would be rational; if rational then necessary; and if necessary, then it would not be sin. But sin is irrational, utterly, and for that reason sin is always represented in the Bible in a symbolical way, for in no other way could it be revealed to us, nor in any other way could we at all understand it. It is transcendental to our present order of existence; does not at all fall within the scope of our existence. Only in this view of the case do we reach the full force and significance of the fall, as being not a letting-down from one plane of existence to another, but an absolute and total fall from one element of existence down into another, which latter has now become a nature to us. This is what we mean by "original sin," which it is always necessary to recognize in order that room may be properly made for the work of redemption.

In these circumstances, our life, thus separated and fallen from God, comes under the dominion of Satan. The world, as fallen, is under the dominion of evil. The fall is an organic ruin, and the redemption from the fall must be an organic redemption.

We have this thought presented in the Gospel Lesson for the day. Christ was casting out a devil. His enemies said, "He casteth out devils through Beelzebub, the chief of the devils." Even they recognized the world as being in some way under the power of the devil. They had no proper conception, however, of the nature either of the devil or of sin. Their declaration that one could "cast out devils by the chief of the devils" is in full line with the humanitarian view, that our fallen humanity carries in its own bosom the remedy for its malady. That is a very false, though a very common view. The world is full of it. Science, art, commerce, political economy—these are forever dreaming of raising man heavenward by his own inherent powers. As over against this, we find in the Scripture lessons assigned for our reading and meditation to-day, an enforcing of the great truth, that a new Power has actually entered into this our fallen world from above and beyond it, by which alone redemption is possible. Men in our Saviour's day were slow to see the great fact, that "The Kingdom of God is come upon you:" that there was an actual historical conflict on the part of Christ with Satan, and a victory over him, in man's behalf and by The Son of Man. We have here, in the Gospel Lesson, a declaration of our Saviour's that He bringing in the Kingdom of God introduces into the world a Kingdom mightier than that of Satan—that He Himself is the stronger Man who will "take from Satan all his armour wherein he trusted, and will divide his spoils."

Then again, with reference to the general thought that nothing short of a new and higher power from above and beyond can ever redeem men, our Lord says, "When the unclean spirit is gone out of a man, he walketh through dry places, seeking rest; and finding none, he saith, I will return unto my house whence I came out. And when he cometh, he findeth it swept and garnished." Here the man, thus newly delivered from evil, is represented as being only what he was before; there has been no change in the spiritual nature. Humanitarianism, at its best estate, can only drive out the unclean spirit, so to speak (if indeed it can do so much as that), and leaves the man much as he was before. His house is "swept and garnished," and there is an outward show of amendment, but no thorough-going, radical change in the inmost sanctuary of the man's soul. "Then goeth he, and taketh to him seven other spirits more wicked than himself: and they enter in and dwell there; and the last state of that man is worse than the first." That is a striking symbolical representation of the great truth, that cannot be too much insisted upon, that there is no help for our fallen humanity from within the bosom of humanity itself. All remedial efforts in the way of art, science, literature, and so forth, must always fail as they always have failed in the past. Though they may even appear for a time to have done good, yet the misery soon comes back again. There has been no relief for our fallen life by civilization, culture, law, politics. These have no power to lift man up and out of his fall. He is in the depths and cannot find his way out by his own power.

"And it came to pass, as he spake these things, a cerwoman of the company lifted up her voice, and said unto him: Blessed is the womb that bare thee, and the paps which thou hast sucked. But he said, Yea rather, blessed are they that hear the Word of God, and keep it"—as much as to say: There has come among men a mighty power from above, even The Word of God, to help and to save. Blessed indeed are they that hear that Word.

Such, then, is the general nature of the fall as set forth in the Gospel Lesson, which seems to gather up into itself the voice out of the abyss into which humanity is fallen, and which is well expressed in the words of the Psalmist, "Out of the depths have I cried unto thee, O Lord." Similarly the collect is a cry of absolute despair of all other help from any other source whatsoever. There is in the human spirit constitutionally a nisus, a struggle after help. We cry out for help. We cannot avoid the feeling that this is not our home; nor can we fail to be sensible of the nothingness and vanity of this our time-existence as over against that ideal existence a conviction of which we carry in our own consciousness, and toward which we are impelled to struggle evermore. And just so far as this is truly felt, so far do we become persuaded of the utter ineffectualness of all human remedies and resources. A man will not cry out of the depths unless he is in absolute extremity.

In such circumstances a cry for help from above must and does involve a measure of faith. In proportion precisely as we feel our extremity, we turn to something greater and higher than ourselves, to something entirely above and beyond ourselves. What that something is we all very well know. God in Christ has come nigh unto us for our salvation and our help. And this approach of God to us is only in Christ. Hence it is that the collect presents this help as coming to us in the way of an organic redemption in the person of Christ, the language of the prayer being that God would mercifully " stretch forth the right hand of His Majesty for our salvation and defense, *through Jesus Christ our Lord.*" If it were not under that character that redemption came into the world, it would be of no avail. The actual descent of a higher life into our fallen life is necessary for our salvation. "No man hath ascended up to heaven, but he that came down from heaven, even the Son of Man which is in heaven." If there was to be an ascension for our poor fallen humanity, there must first of all be a descension of the Son of Man into the very bosom of it. The relation between the two is not arbitrary but necessary. We can see the operation of that law even in the world of nature, where each lower system is universally suspended and dependent upon systems and powers above. What would Christ after all have been for us, what could He have been for us, had He been only a man? Had He been so He would not have been "The strong Man" attacking Satan and overcoming him.

All this, now, is involved in that cry of faith out of the depths. And in this way, by such an exercise of faith in the mighty Deliverer, we are brought to an actual part and participation in a real victory over Satan. We are to be delivered, not merely from disease and the other sure consequences of sin, but first of all from our nature of sin. Men talk of the new birth—but what does this mean if not the actual insertion of the subject into the very life of Christ? This translation into Christ is a lifting up of the soul out of this fallen element into a higher element. This is a transcendental act, as was the introduction of sin into the world, and the fall. The feeling of such a translation of our fallen life into a higher sphere was very strong, evidently, in the early Church, and was very beautifully represented by the symbol of a fish, which symbol was no doubt originally suggested by the declaration of our Lord that He would make His disciples "Fishers of Men." No other symbol was more generally known, or more universally esteemed in the early Church, than this, excepting the cross, the primitive Christians seeing in the letters composing the Greek name for a fish a very beautiful signification. To their mind it seemed that even as a fish is raised out of the cold dark element of the water into the clear, warm element of the air, even so are we in Christ raised up to a new and higher life. This symbol may, indeed, strike some as absurd, forasmuch as they see not the force of the fall of man.

The practical use of these reflections is plain enough,

and is well brought out in the Epistle Lesson. If we have been thus raised out of the depths, we are to live in a manner answerable to this new and higher life. We are to be " followers of God, as dear children, and to walk in love, as Christ also hath loved us." The peculiarity of the Gospel and Epistle exhortations against sin is this, that they proceed upon the presupposition of an actual order of new life into which believers are regarded as having been raised. Those who were in that lower dark order are now in the higher. Nothing is said of their experience. They have passed over into the kingdom of light, and they are evermore to walk worthy of the exalted position they have been permitted, by the grace of God, to occupy.

March 3d, 1872.

The Fourth Sunday in Lent.

THE WAY OF THE TRANSGRESSOR.

Proverbs xiii. 15.

"The way of transgressors is hard."

THE way of transgressors is hard because it is a wrong way, and one that is injurious to others as well as to the transgressor himself: and the text may have reference to this latter aspect of the case. Transgression sooner or later is followed by a sense of contradiction and conflict with the regularly constituted order of things, and must eventually be attended with pain and suffering.

It is easy enough to see that the way of trangression is hard for the sinner himself, even though it may be difficult at first to see how that way should involve hardship for others. It is clear that the sinner must suffer; it is clear from the very nature of transgression. Transgression is a going beyond the mark, an exceeding of the boundaries by which the proper conception of life is defined and limited. The root conception of it is a going beyond the mark, a going astray from the right. All such excess and transgression must be visited with penalty. It is as if a man on a journey, or going from place to place, proposes some point to himself, and then wanders out of the way, goes into fields and forests. Such a man of necessity will lose much valuable time, will make the way hard for himself, will find his journey attended with difficulty, and will ultimately fail of reaching his desired end.

Just so it is in the moral world. To go out of the way is at once to be involved in difficulty, hardship and pain. We are shut up to this conclusion so soon as we admit that there is a divine order of things in the world at all. Any violation of that order must bring pain. The hardness of the sinner's way thus comes into view when we see that the transgressor sets himself in contradiction both to the purpose of his own life and the purpose of the life of the world around him.

The way of the transgressor is hard, not only because he must eventually suffer, when society, or violated law, takes vengeance on him for his transgression, it may be many years after the sin was done. That is true; but there is something more than that. His punishment begins from the very moment of his transgression. He can't escape the sense of violation and contradiction from the very outstart. His way is hard from the beginning to the end. That is what we mean by conscience—a voice, or power within the man pronouncing condemnation upon him. So long as he is involved in transgression his way must be hard. His condition is that of the wicked, who are "like the troubled sea, when it cannot rest, whose waters cast up mire and dirt. There is no peace, saith my God, to the wicked."

This connects itself with the further thought, that the way of the transgressor comes into contradiction and conflict with the consciences and the lives of men around him, all of whom stand in one common moral life, not by any consent or conventionality, or agreement on their part, but by constitutional necessity underlying the whole social economy. Any trangression or violation of the moral law thus constitutionally involved, must be followed by punishment. Public sentiment will not be slow to resent the wrong, and to punish the wrong-doer. So long as the transgressor lives in society he must suffer hardship and pain. His suffering may arise merely from the feeling that his neighbor condemns him, or that the general public opinion does so, or it may result from a sentence formally pronounced by the civil law. This social system we see at work everywhere guarding against transgression, and everywhere making the way of transgressors hard.

But the misery does not end here. The moral grounds itself always in the physical. Both systems proceed from God as their common source; both must agree, and both must have one common end. It cannot be otherwise than that trangression should be visited by physical punishment for violations of the moral law. The sinner may indeed flourish like the green bay tree for a certain time; but sooner or later the moral law will demand satisfaction. In many forms of transgression, the powers of nature themselves punish the sinner. The drunkard, the licentious man, and others like them, suffer the inevitable physical consequences of their degrading vices. These consequences do not come upon them merely by accident, but by a natural, physical necessity. The way of these transgressors is hard. Their punishment is of a vindicatory character; becomes a divine nemesis, relentlessly, remorselessly pursuing the evil-doer. The sinner, like Cain, has a mark set upon him, and bears the shameful brand of his sin on his very face. Such vindicatory punishment is not confined to these low and sensual forms of trangression. It extends throughout the whole social and moral economy, and keeps steady pace with the character of the transgression, too; so that the more deeply the sinner strikes at the heart of the moral law, the more fiercely is he pursued and the more severely is he punished.

In this way we can see what must be the relation of the physical world to the sinner. All its powers will be arrayed against him. The very stones cry out for his punishment, and the far-away stars witness against him. All the powers of nature are all the time crying out for his destruction. At last the man can no longer withstand the crushing weight of violated law; he is overwhelmed; and so sinks into his grave.

But this is not yet all. There is a worse punishment still in store for the transgressor. Our present life is only a preparation for a future world. Our existence here is only transient and temporary. The evidence of this meets us on all sides. At the same time we become aware that the present order and constitution of the world cannot, as we have seen, be violated without certain punishment following, and that it assumes a vindicatory character. Yet on the other hand we also see exceptional failures of justice. The sinner is not always overtaken in his evil way. The wicked do sometimes flourish like the green bay tree. What shall we say to this? Shall we say that such facts go to show that God's order in the world is a failure, because we cannot see exactly how it is that not all men are punished in the degree of their guilt and after the merits of their transgression?

No, God's government of this world is strictly moral; but His government of men here is only partial and temporary. The present order of things looks forward to a higher order. The existence of men in this world is preliminary to their existence in the other world, and there in that other world there must be an ultimate harmony, through the full punishment of sinners to the full extent of their merits—to the full extent of that which is typified in these shadowy punishments here in this world. And it is chiefly in view of this final retribution in a future state that we can see the full force and significance of the declaration of the text that, "The way of transgressors is hard."

"The wicked shall perish." "Thine enemies shall perish." Such is the repeated declaration of the Psalmist. There is an absolute certainty that they shall. There is something terrible in the mere form in which punishment is so repeatedly denounced in Scripture against the wicked. Such punishment, in God's moral government of the world, is universal, absolute, necessary. In view of these facts, that "The way of transgressors is hard," but that "The path of the just is as a light shining more and more unto the perfect day," we should endeavor to make our calling and election sure.

March 27, 1870.

The Sixth Sunday in Lent—Palm Sunday.

SUFFERING AND REIGNING.

The Epistle Lesson for the Day.—Philippians ii. 5–11.

"Let this mind be in you, which was also in Christ Jesus: who, being in the form of God, thought it not robbery to be equal with God; but made himself of no reputation, and took upon him the form of a servant, and was made in the likeness of men; and being found in fashion as a man, he humbled himself, and became obedient unto death, even the death of the cross."

UNDER what particular view this exhortation is given may be seen in the concluding words of the collect: "That we may be counted worthy to have part, both in the fellowship of His sufferings, and in the glorious power of His resurrection."

This may be regarded as the leading theme of Palm Sunday, which looks to Good Friday as preparatory to the resurrection of our Lord. We have the same idea in the Gospel for the day, brought into view by the character of Christ's entrance into Jerusalem: "Fear not, daughter of Zion: behold, thy King cometh, sitting on an ass' colt." The theme of the Gospel is the same as that of the Epistle, viz., the contrast between the humiliation of Christ and His glorification thereafter following.

The humiliation of Christ begins in His birth, and reaches on through His life to His burial and descent into Hades. There is a certain amount of analogy between the occasion of His entrance into Jerusalem and His entrance upon His work, when He was tempted in the wilderness. In that temptation the Saviour, in the solitude of His spirit, met the great problem of His life. His determination was made in a resolute way then, and His whole subsequent public life and ministry were in conformity with this resolution. His life was throughout a conflict between two worlds—between light and darkness. As He came into the world to redeem it, He could do so only in the way of conflict. All His miracles and teachings bring to view the opposition of these two worlds, as well as certain glimpses, at the same time, of His ultimate victory and future glorification. But, notwithstanding these glimpses, His life was preeminently one of humiliation.

The occasion of His last entrance into Jerusalem brings these two worlds into striking contrast. In His temptation the conflict was private; here it was exposed to the view of the world. There were glimpses and prophecies of His glorification, as in the transfiguration, and in the coming of certain Greeks to Him in the temple. But these were only transient, however. The Messianic hopes of the Jewish world were dashed by that declaration of His, "Except a corn of wheat fall into the ground and die, it abideth alone." The disciples themselves were ever and always made to feel that the Kingdom belonged to another order entirely, above and beyond this world.

On this occasion we have, as it were, a still brighter promise of what was to come. The feeling of the coming of the Kingdom had been growing among the people, and among the strangers now at Jerusalem and on their way to the feast, there was a more or less intense conviction that the Kingdom was now nigh at hand. They were eagerly awaiting a Redeemer to come to their help and deliverance, expecting Him in a temporal way, and after a worldly fashion. They imagined that He would place Himself at their head in a political way. So strong had this feeling grown that some time previously, on the occasion of the miraculous feeding of the five thousand, He had found it necessary to withdraw beyond the sea, "lest they come and take Him by force and make him a king." Here, on this occasion, we find this same feeling manifested again, heightened and intensified, no doubt, also, by the recent raising of Lazarus from the dead.

Multitudes hailed Him from the walls and gates of Jerusalem, and multitudes shouted " Hosanna " as they moved along in procession by His side. It was a brilliant display of popular enthusiasm, and may be regarded as in some sort a temptation for Christ, as was the proffer of all the kingdoms of this world by the Evil One in the wilderness. This feeling was grounded, no doubt, in a right disposition, but was worldly, for they imagined that the time had now at length come for Him to declare and manifest Himself as their king in a worldly way. The hour was now near at hand for His glorification. At Cana He said, " Mine hour is not yet come." And at the feeding of the five thousand His hour had not yet come. But now, after the miracle of raising Lazarus from the dead, and after the Pharisees had counselled and determined to put Him to death, He comes out from His retirement and yields Himself for a time to this popular feeling, though He felt that it would yield to another end entirely than that they had in view. He yields to this popular enthusiasm, neither gratifying nor condemning it, but regarding it as necessary in order to precipitate the designs of the Pharisees, that through it He might defeat all such expectations forever, and so come to the light and glorification of His resurrection from the dead.

In this way we can see how this historical passage in the Saviour's life serves to symbolize the humiliation and subsequent glorification of His whole life and work.

The Epistle now bases itself on the consideration of the glorification of Christ as something already at hand. We have also strongly brought out, in this same Epistle, the infinite humiliation of Christ. It goes back to the incarnation, and views the humiliation from that standpoint. The laying aside of the glory of the Logos is an act into which the angels desire to look. The original for " made Himself of no reputation " is " He emptied Himself" (ἑαυτὸν ἐκένωσε). What that means we need not here at length consider. But we are to remember that the incarnation was not a mere theophany. It involved, according to the language here employed, an emptying of deity. The union of the Word with humanity was actual and real, and passed successively through all the conditions of our life, birth, development, growth, trial, temptation, involving the necessity of prayer as really as that of food and rest. His life was an actual human trial; it must have been so, in order that there might be also for our humanity in Him an actual victory.

" He thought it not robbery to be equal with God "— better, " He did not pertinaciously cleave to His divinity," but parted with it, emptied Himself of it, " and was made in the likeness of men "—that is, in the actual form of man.

That is the first part of the humiliation of the Son of God. But that is not all. Having taken on Him our nature, He entered upon our earthly life of humiliation, and in the full spirit of obedience to authority, " He became obedient unto death, even unto the death of the cross."

In this brief way the Apostle brings into view the humiliation that he may contrast with it the following glorification. We cannot at all understand the latter without the former. The two are mutually conditional. "*Wherefore* God also hath highly exalted him, and given him a name which is above every name." Observe, also, that this exaltation of Christ is here presented not merely as the exaltation of the Logos; for as the Logos He had glory with the Father before the world was. It is the exaltation and glorification of *the world in Him*. He passed through the world, and bore it with Him and in His own person in triumph up to heaven.

It is here that the Lesson for the day comes into view. The humiliation is followed by glorification, not primarily, however, by way of reward, though that is in it, too, but not in any outward way merely, as depending on the mind of God, but as necessarily involved as an unfailing consequence. The glorification, above and beyond the fact that it is a reward by virtue of inward constition and relationship, is furthermore the necessary result of the whole life of Christ, and this is the matter of chief importance here. The glorification of Christ is never appreciated properly, except as it is seen to be an actual victory of Christ, beginning in His birth in Bethlehem and resulting finally in His ascension from Olivet. This victory, in the nature of the case, could not be secured from without but only from within humanity. The victory must be accomplished in the very bosom of our life, and somehow by the very powers of our life. For that reason Jesus tabernacled in the flesh for three and thirty years, and endured all its sufferings. He could not have the victory standing apart from our life, beyond it or above it. He must be in humanity in its deepest ground, joining Himself to it by a holy conception of the Virgin. The Kingdom of Christ thus involves a complete victory in the world. He grappled with the world forces in their historical form, and passed by the transition through death and resurrection over into a higher order. His glorification is His victory, as the necessary result of His life.

We are called on to-day to contemplate this example. The victory of Christ thus considered is not a victory outside the world, but one that is now and here present in it. It is here repeating itself in the believer, both in the form of humiliation and in that of glorification. As these could not be separated in Christ, so neither can they in the believer. There is but one law for the Master and for the disciple. That is grounded in the very constitution of our being. St. Paul earnestly desired to have fellowship in the sufferings of Christ. He wished to have part not primarily in His glory, but in His sufferings, saying, "If we suffer we shall also reign with Him." We cannot have the latter without the former. If we are in earnest we will covet a part in the sufferings of Christ, the idea of the true Christian life being not merely that we should submit to them, but rather that we should court them, for then are we nearest to the cross of our Lord. In the absence of all worldly hope and confidence, then it is that Christ comes nearest to us. That is the use we should make of this whole occasion for the purpose of our own personal profit as believing souls, as we see in the collect, where we pray that " we may be counted worthy to have part both in the fellowship of His sufferings, and in the glorious power of His resurrection."

We notice, briefly, one more thought—that the life of Christ running through His whole work, and coming out here especially in this cry of " Hosanna," is a type of our life. We are so apt to look on the world in its outward progress as working out in some certain way the end of human life. Such is the belief and the boast of the world. And the tendency of the Church nowaday is to make a compromise with the world's vain hope and expectation in this way. The world can never, in the true sense of the word, glorify itself, much less can it ever glorify the Church. The course of our Saviour's ministry, starting in the temptation in the wilderness and ending here in the experiences of Palm Sunday as preparatory to Good Friday, we cannot at all properly contemplate without feeling that in the consciousness of Christ at least (and what a consciousness that was!) the world is now and forever must remain utterly and hopelessly incapable of leading itself up by its own power to its own glorification.

March 24, 1872.

The First Sunday after Easter.

"THE GLORIOUS PRINCE OF SALVATION."

Hebrews ii. 10.

" For it became him, for whom are all things, and by whom are all things, in bringing many sons unto glory, to make the captain of their salvation perfect through sufferings."

THE words, "the captain of their salvation," are in the original 'Αρχηγὸς τῆς σωτηρίας αὐτῶν. The meaning of the word here rendered "captain," is not fully expressed by that term. The idea is rather that of a path-finder, or a breaker-of-the-way—like a prince leading his people and opening the way for them to follow.

The redemption of the world in Christ is not something magical or abrupt. It is no after-thought entering into the divine mind for the first time at a certain stage in the world's progress, but stands in the scheme of the world and of human history from the beginning. That scheme included the fall and the remedy for the fall. There is a close connexion between the work of redemption and the work of creation. We can easily see that relation when we consider that redemption will work a change not only in the stream of history, but reaches out to the physical world of nature as well, not having attained its glorious consummation until it has introduced "the new heavens and earth wherein dwelleth righteousness." The last times will involve a vast change not only in the moral but also in the physical world. Standing thus between creation on the one hand, and the end of all things on the other, we can easily see that redemption is nothing magical or abrupt, but stands in intimate relation with the law of human history, with the plan or scheme of the world considered as a whole.

This, the cosmical relation of redemption, as we may call it, was evidently in the mind of the writer at the time of writing, as we see in the words, "For it became him, for whom are all things, and by whom are all things, in bringing many sons unto glory, to make the captain of their salvation perfect through sufferings." There was a necessity that Christ should suffer, that He should be the way-breaker, the leader and prince of our humanity in suffering. There was a necessity and a reason for a crucified Saviour. The declaration of the text is that the way could not be made open for others except by Christ going before. Then, also, it implies that there was but one way in which that great leader could go—there was no other way—and that was the way of suffering. There could be no magic about it, such as the ancient gnostics, for example, conceived our Lord's person and sufferings to have been, resolving all into a mere show or magical appearance. There was a necessity in the case not only for a way-breaker, or captain, but for one that was real and not visionary. It was not possible that such a gnostic captain of salvation could save, because the barriers which lay between us and God were not fantastic but real, consisting of the kingdom of Satan, which is a real and not an imaginary or figurative kingdom. That this latter is a real power shows itself plainly enough in the fact that its might reaches not only into the world of intelligence but also into that of nature, for man grows out of nature through his body, and his constitution is such that if he as an intelligent being falls, nature falls with him. "By one man sin entered into the world, and death by sin." The evil and the ruin reached through man's spiritual nature down into the lower physical side of his being. And death, as the result of sin, is something real also, exerting a physical power. When all nature is, by the Apostle, said to be "groaning and travailing in pain"—it is not a mere figure of speech but a sober statement of fact.

All this is implied in our text. It is not enough that sin should be pardoned and the will rectified. There must be more than that. The law of the curse lying on the world must be removed or overcome, by a creative force going down as deep as the curse. Redemption not only takes away sin, but abolishes death, overcomes Hades. These must be broken, abolished. And there was only one way in which that could be done. It could not be accomplished by the establishment of an outward earthly kingdom, nor yet by the assistance and co-operation of merely humanitarian efforts. There is no healing or helping of our poor humanity which leaves it in the bosom and on the plane of this life, leaving death not overcome and the curse still unbroken. To what would all that amount? If there were to be any release at all, it must of necessity be by death, by going down to the very ground and foundation of the curse. If there were to be any path broken, the path-finder must himself endure suffering. Men could not be saved as it were by a stroke from heaven. It was not enough that such a deliverer should merely seem to stand among men, and appear to suffer, and then abruptly and suddenly fly away again to the heavens, leaving only a sham deliverance behind him. He could not thus be the captain of salvation. He must suffer death, go down into Hades, destroy death and rise superior to both. He became perfect for Himself; for when He stood among us He could not relieve Himself of the situation in which He was, save only by carrying our humanity in His own person triumphantly through the gates and bars of death.

We can see, in this way, wherein consisted the necessity of suffering for our great captain of salvation. It was necessary that He should suffer in order that righteousness and life might be obtained for us. But we are to remember that this necessity was not a merely outward necessity. He must suffer in order to be true to Himself, and in order that He might be a way-breaker that others might follow in the pathway He had opened—by which we do not mean that others should do what He did, for He alone of all the sons of Adam broke the way through sin, death and hell.

It is also implied here that there never was, is not now nor ever can be any other prince of salvation, or any other way of escape from sin and death. If before Christ's day no other way could be found, certainly none could be found after. "I am the way, the truth and the life," says our Saviour. And again "No man cometh unto the Father but by me." "Neither is there salvation in any other," says St. Peter, "for there is none other name under heaven, given among men, whereby we must be saved." If we wish to gain heaven, there is only one thing for us to do—choose Him for our leader and captain and prince of salvation, and to follow in His footsteps over that way trodden by the feet of that vast and glorious army of the saints looking down upon us from the battlements of heaven as witnesses of our christian course. We may, indeed, look to these witnesses and consider their good and godly example, for our encouragement, but above all are we to "look to Jesus, the author and finisher of our faith, who for the joy that was set before Him, endured the cross, despising the shame, and is now set down at the right hand of the throne of God."

Furthermore, we are all assured that the way is now open, the path broken, the enemy conquered, death slain, Satan bound. In these circumstances of victory by the Son of Man, we are all called upon to consider for our encouragement the high vantage ground upon which our feet are placed. We are called upon to make our calling and election sure. There is, thus, much that is truly animating and inspiring in the text—but there is in it much of warning too. As the writer of this epistle says in the opening words of this chapter—"Therefore we ought to give the more earnest heed to the things which we have heard, lest at any time we should let them slip. For if the word spoken by angels was steadfast, and every transgression and disobedience received a just recompense of reward, how shall we escape if we neglect so great salvation?" And then the same writer goes on to add:—"But one in a certain place testified, saying, What is man that thou art mindful of him, or the son of man that thou visitest him? Thou madest him a little lower than the angels, . . . Thou hast put all things under his feet . . . But now we see not yet all things put under him"—(indeed, the reverse is true; for instead of having the world under him, man in his fallen state is under the world, and under Satan; so that man's state and condition is full of discouragement)—"But we see Jesus"—(who has conquered, and gathered up the broken fortunes of humanity)—"who was made a little lower than the angels for the suffering of death"—(not remaining bound under the power of death, but arising out of and ascending above and beyond it, and so opening the way)—" crowned with glory and honor "—(not for Himself only, but for sinners)—" that he by the grace of God should taste death for every man,"—and thus take away the sting of death for all who follow Him in the way of the Gospel.

April 23, 1870.

The Second Sunday after Easter.

SEEING THE FATHER.

John xiv. 9.

"*Jesus said unto him, Have I been so long time with you, and yet hast thou not known me, Philip? He that hath seen me, hath seen the Father; and how sayest thou then, Shew us the Father?*"

OF the being of God in His absolute character we can form no conception whatever, for the reason that such a conception would involve a limitation of a Being who is illimitable, forasmuch as He is the infinite God. It is by limiting and bounding things that we can apprehend them with the understanding. God in His absolute character cannot be apprehended by the finite mind; a fact which was understood by the heathen writers who uniformly spoke of Him as absolute, separate existence, without limitation or confinement. Sometimes God is spoken of by them as "The Abyss," or as "Silence," conveying the idea that God in His absolute nature cannot be apprehended by the finite mind. If we do attempt anything of this kind, we get only a negative conception at best. We say, God is infinite—that is He is not bounded as to space. Or, again, we say, God is eternal—that is, He is not bounded as to time.

So then we cannot have any apprehension of God in the way of the understanding. There is another way, however, in which God may make Himself apprehensible, so as to come into union with our being, namely, in the way of a revelation—a coming out of this darkness and abyss. Revelation universally, and in the widest sense of the word, is an act of God by which He manifests Himself in such a way, or under such conditions, as that He may be seen and understood, relatively but not absolutely, by an intelligent person. Under this view it is that the Scriptures speak of the revelation of God. They represent Him as being utterly beyond all apprehension, so far as mere subjective human effort is concerned. "Canst thou by searching find out God?" it is said in the book of Job: "Canst thou find out the Almighty unto perfection? It is as high as heaven, what canst thou do? it is deeper than hell, what canst thou know?"

Yet, at the same time, under another view, it is also said in the Scriptures that we may know God. "This is eternal life that they might know thee and Jesus Christ whom thou hast sent." Many passages might be quoted in which it is said that God may be known, under the view of a revelation. And that revelation which God has been pleased to make of Himself for our human world (we know not how it may be in other worlds, and with beings differently constituted) presents itself under different forms more or less relative.

I. The first and most immediate revelation He has made of Himself is in the world of nature: which however would be of no account without something further. It would not be complete, or of any account at all, without our human nature. Nature is represented in the Scripture as a book for study, it may be not for us alone: it may be for the angels quite as well as for us, for aught we know. "Day unto day uttereth speech, and night unto night showeth knowledge." The very stars in their courses speak out His praises. St. Paul, in the first chapter of the Epistle to the Romans says, that, "The invisible things of him from the creation of the world are clearly seen, being understood by the things that are made, even his eternal power and Godhead:" and he then goes on to show the sin of the heathen world in not acknowledging His existence, and in falling away from the worship of God, to that of the creature.

II. Now, however, as we have said, the revelation becomes effective only as taken in connection with the presence of intelligent and self-conscious being. Mind must be present to serve as a mirror to make nature intelligible; and the only way that we can see that to be possible, is by supposing there to be an original, eternal harmony between the outward world of nature and the inner world of mind, by virtue of which the outward carries this sense from the beginning, so that it may be reflected by the thought of man. These two, the world of nature and the world of mind, are constitutionally one, as two hemispheres of the same globe, or as two opposite, though mutually complementing parts of the same great creative scheme or plan. There is the same reason—in different forms, of course—in both, both proceeding from the hand of the same God. Nature wakes up to a consciousness of herself in man. We can thus see that what is sometimes spoken of as "a revelation of God in the world of nature" takes a far higher form when it comes to be a revelation of God in the constitution of the human mind. There we have a revelation of God far surpassing any possible revelation in the world of nature. "There is a spirit in man: and the inspiration of the Almighty giveth them understanding." The divine spirit and the human are so related that it is not possible for the human to unfold itself so as to understand itself and nature without involving, at the same time, a revelation of God. In such a revelation (in the human constitution, namely) we have the presence of God in a measure far beyond what it is in nature: for here we meet the development of the will, and enter the ethical sphere. And as this is not at all possible below man, the revelation moves on a far higher plane, and is correspondingly greater and more glorious than it can be in any sphere below that of man. In nature we see God's revelation physically: in man we see God's revelation ethically. In man the revelation unfolds itself in the form of history. Here we meet something grander and greater far than the voice of God speaking to us in the tones of the thunder or in the sparkling stars in the heavens above, for here we are listening to God speaking to us in the voice of the ages.

III. Without dwelling upon this any longer, I proceed to say that the only full, complete, and the highest possible revelation that God can make of Himself is the revelation that has been made in sending Christ into the world. He became flesh of our flesh, and bone of our bone, and so entered the stream of our human life, as to become the centre of its power. This mode of revelation, however, cannot be said to bring out the whole sense of God's absolute being for our apprehension, yet as compared with the former, it brings God into contact with us in a way that is not possible through either the world of nature or the world of mind. This form of revelation is not to be taken merely in the sense of something intellectual, as if it were only a certain amount of instruction as to the being and the attributes of God. Neither must we regard it as a simple addition to other methods or schemes of revelation, as if Christ came merely to give us more knowledge than we can find either in nature, or in that revelation which God made in earlier ages, by the agency of Moses, for example. Such a revelation would be, at best, only the old revelation under a higher form. The revelation of God in Christ must be regarded as having been from the very beginning, not in the way of teaching, but of being. Unless we reach that thought we never can understand either history or nature, nor the meaning of the text, " He that hath seen me "—not merely with the outward sense. It is true, sense-perception was the necessary medium for the revelation of His glory, but nevertheless the revelation was not taken in by the outward eye alone, for multitudes saw Him, and viewed Him merely as a common man, and did not at all see the Father in Him, but crucified Him between two thieves. Even in perceiving any object in nature, the outward form of the object and the sense of the beholder mediate the spiritual communication between the two; but in order to a true communion with the object there must be something more and something deeper than a mere sense-perception.

When our Lord said to Philip, " He that hath seen me hath seen the Father," He did not mean to say, " He that hath come to understand my higher nature in the way of intellectual observation." God could not be seen even by Moses by sense observation: and He never has been and never can be seen by merely intellectual observation. There must be something deeper. The mind may indeed go very far in the way of intellectual speculation as to what is necessarily involved in the being and attributes of God, but to what does all that amount? It did not amount to very much, in the case of Philip here, at all events. He was embarrassed, and said to Christ, "Shew us the Father." Who is He? Where is He? What relation does He sustain to Thee, and to us? Our Saviour plainly did not mean, by His reply, to say that knowledge of Him consisted in His *teaching :* for Philip and the other disciples knew hardly anything as compared with the great theologians of later days; for the work of redemption had not yet been wrought out, there had been no descent into Hades, no resurrection, no ascension and glorification. The fact that our Lord said these things under these circumstances shows plainly enough that the knowledge of Him was possible for Philip and the other disciples and did not require such great intellectual power. On the contrary it implies that they had known Him before this, and did so know Him then.

The organ of such knowledge was faith. Only thus can this revelation of God in Christ come to any man. Only so did it come to those who actually saw Christ with the eyes of the body. That revelation authenticated itself to them. Why did the disciples believe in Him? Because God in Christ had so taken hold of them that they were overwhelmed with sorrow at the thought of separation from Him.

"He that hath seen me hath seen the Father." That is the only way man can see the Father. That never can be, as some have dreamed, through the medium of our human life made commensurate with the ideal. In the person of Christ we have not merely an idealized humanity, but a humanity joined to divinity, and a revelation therefore of God in man. It was not simply such a revelation as that God makes of Himself in the storm, the ocean, the stars, the cataract, or even such as is found in history. No doctrine, no speculation, however wisely or however far conducted, can ever mount up to the dignity, the sublime majesty of such a revelation as is here meant. The revelation must be joined to our very life, actually, and not in the way of mere theory. It was undoubtedly for this reason that Christ came into organic, vital, concrete union with our life, and thus made an intelligent apprehension of the Father possible to us, as was seen after His resurrection, and will be fully realized only in His second coming.

There are different degrees of such seeing. The only true knowledge of God becomes possible to us only in so far as we are inserted into this higher life, and grow up in His likeness. When we come to look at the text in this way, we see how absurd was this request of Philip, though it came from a pure and simple mind. "Shew us the Father," said he. How could God be known except in Christ? All other ways of knowing God are utterly of no account, as set over against the living apprehension of Him in His Son, who is "the brightness of His glory, and the express image of His person."

Many practical reflections follow naturally from this course of thought, but I shall notice, briefly only two—

I. In a declaration of this kind, which is only one of hundreds of similar import, we have a direct argument for the divinity of Christ, the force of which goes far beyond that of any texts considered as addressed merely to the understanding, or as addressed to men outside of the christian sphere, to be interpreted merely by the intellect. Such texts, considered as thus addressed, can carry no weight as compared with this. We have many texts like the one under consideration, and what is remarkable about them is their consistent harmony. "No man knoweth the Son but the Father; neither knoweth any man the Father save the Son, and he to whomsoever the Son will reveal Him." "He that hath seen me hath seen the Father; how sayest thou then, shew us the Father?" How can you doubt for a moment what our Saviour held in His own consciousness? Could He have used language at all like this unless He intended to assert His divinity?

II. The thought of the original, constitutional and eternal kinship between our mind and the divine mind. We cannot think of the Incarnation as a Hindoo Avatar, God taking the form of one animal now and another then. There cannot be any incarnation where the two natures to be joined are incongruous. The original relationship between God and man is such that salvation was possible. This is a great thought, without the help of which we are likely to go astray in our theological thinking. When we look to the stars, "What is man that thou art mindful of him, or the Son of Man that thou visitest him?" But what is this manifestation of God as compared with that revelation He has made in Christ? There it is that the full dignity of our human life appears. Let us not count ourselves unworthy, or be neglectful, of so great a revelation and salvation. To them that count themselves so, well may we apply the language of the proverb—"Wherefore is the price of wisdom in the hand of a fool?" "See that ye receive not the grace of God in vain."

May 1, 1870.

The Fifth Sunday after Easter.

THE BELIEVER'S CROWN OF LIFE.

Revelation iii. 11.

"*Behold, I come quickly; hold that fast which thou hast, that no man take thy crown.*"

THE crown has been in every age a symbol of victory. We may regard the crown referred to in this passage of Scripture, either as a crown of nature or as a crown of grace, or better still as involving both the one and the other. The former conception attaches to our human existence from its very beginning. Man is the crown of nature, as we see in the account given of the creation in the first chapters of Genesis. All nature comes to its completion in man—which could not at all be the case, however, except by reason of its unity with the spirit of man. A declaration of this underlying unity we find in the account of the creation of man as given in Genesis: "And the Lord God formed man of the dust of the ground, and breathed into his nostrils the breath of life: and man became a living soul." As thus constituted man may be said to have been crowned from the beginning with glory and majesty, as is said in the book of the Psalms, "For thou hast made him a little lower than the angels, and hast crowned him with glory and honor. Thou hast made him to have dominion over the works of thy hands: thou hast put all things under his feet."

This crown stood directly in the spirit of man, as made in the image and likeness of God. He was designed by his very constitution to be the prophet, priest and king of the creation below him.

The order, however, as instituted in the time of man's innocency, was not kept, and is now abnormal. The Psalmist indeed says, "Thou hast put all things under his feet;" but the author of the Epistle to the Hebrews, in commenting on this passage, says, "We see not yet all things put under him, but we see Jesus who was made a little lower than the angels for the suffering of death, crowned with glory and honor." In the present disorganized state consequent upon sin, such is the relation between man and the world of nature that, instead of being her lord and sovereign, man is a prey to her forces and powers, and eventually succumbs to death.

But in Christ Jesus the lofty position, for which our nature was designed by the Creator, has been regained. In Him the race has been recapitulated—it has received a new headship in Him, as it is said in Ephesians i. 10— " That in the dispensation of the fulness of the times he might gather together in one all things in Christ (or, might recapitulate or re-head all things in Him) both which are in heaven and which are on earth." And again, in the twenty-second verse of the same chapter it is said, "And hath put all things under his feet, and gave him to be the head over all things to the church." Being, in this way the new, living, organic Head of the race, all that original dignity of our nature, of which we have been speaking, holds first of all in the person of Christ, and is restored to those who are in union with His divine-human life in the spirit. On the day of Pentecost, the Holy Ghost, who thus far in our Lord's ministry had been confined to His own person, and who previously had not been given "because Jesus was not yet glorified," became universal in the scope and power of His blessed operations among the dying sons of men, in making them partakers of the new higher life introduced into the world by "the second Adam, the Lord from heaven."

"Let no man take from thee thy crown," now, has reference to this. The crown had fallen into the dust, as it were, but is now again lifted up out of its unseemly degradation. The two crowns (of nature and of grace) are not related externally or magically. It is perfectly plain from the teachings of the New Testament that the two creations, the natural and the supernatural, proceed from one common origin and source, The Logos, and there can be no contradiction, therefore, between the crown of nature and the crown of grace. The exhortation, "Hold fast that which thou hast, that no man take thy crown," should not be regarded, consequently, as having to do only with the one or the other, exclusively or mainly, but should be considered as applying to both in that close inner relationship holding between the two.

Notice the emphasis evidently intended to be laid upon the word "thy." It is, "*Thy* crown." There is here a present, personal possession. "Hold that fast which thou *hast*"—the crown that belongs to thee as thine own right and property. So far as the dignity of our nature is properly held to, even though we are fallen, we are required to hold fast our crown. There is a false view of the fall according to which man has lost all dignity in the scale of being, all possibility of salvation. Capacities of looking up to God we still have, and hold in our inmost consciousness. The crown is indeed fallen into the dust, but it is not lost. "There is a spirit in man, and the inspiration of the Almighty giveth them understanding." What is there in all the world that can in any way compete with the glorious possession of this great dignity, this heavenward tendency of the spirit of man? How poor, how vain, how mean and unsatisfying is all in comparison beside!

But these lofty aspirations may be repressed. The rational nature may not be allowed to assert itself. The meaning of one's personality may not be honored in its great and high claims. "Hold that fast which thou hast," therefore; make due account of your intelligent nature; master all earthly sympathies, affections and passions in the service of this your high and immortal calling.

The full force and meaning of the text however, appears only when it is considered to refer to the christian crown of grace. Here there is also a personal, present possession. Those addressed by the text are regarded as having been already brought into union with Christ, first of all in their baptism, and then, on the ground and basis of this, in their own subjective, personal participation in Christ and all His benefits. There is, of course, no power in baptism to save without a personal appropriating activity. The exhortation is not, "Seek that which thou hast not yet obtained," but "Hold that fast which thou hast." The address is made to christians, as having something of unspeakable value. Honor your baptism. Let no one persuade you to depreciate its value, as if it had no meaning or force. Not only our baptism, however, but also our whole christian experience constitute our priceless crown of grace.

There is a possibility of losing this crown. As a man may sink his rational nature in that which is lower, so also may he lose the force and power of his baptism by an irreligious and wicked life.

Observe the independent activity of the subject as being able to prevent this loss, or robbery. "Hold that fast which thou hast"—*let* no man take away thy crown. We cannot be robbed of our intelligence or moral consciousness in a merely outward way by the will of another, not even when such robbery should go the full length of our physical destruction. We may be deprived of our property, our material possessions in that way, but that which pertains to our personality cannot be alienated save by our consent and co-operation. We may be killed by the will of another, but we may not be robbed of any of our spiritual possessions except by our own will. In view of this, what a tremendous force and meaning there is in the exhortation, Let no man take away thy crown! thy crown of nature, thy crown of grace, thine imperishable, inalienable birthright as an immortal man!

Regeneration is not, indeed, a standing, fixed possession, but a continual influx or flow of gracious life into the soul from powers above and beyond. A man's christian life is not his property as a horse is. What then is he to do, if this is not his property? Shall he sit still and do nothing, overpowered by the idea of his helplessness? Not at all! We are to hold our spirits in right relation constantly, and keep them always open and receptive to this gracious life coming down from above. Man has that power. Intelligence does not govern the will, but the will governs intelligence. Our Saviour says, "The light of the body is the eye: if therefore thine eye be single, thy whole body shall be full of light; but if thine eye be evil, thy whole body shall be full of darkness. If therefore the light that is in thee be darkness, how great is that darkness!" That profound declaration of our Saviour's, which looks so far down into the moral and spiritual depths of man's nature, shows clearly enough that there is nothing magical or fatalistic in the possession or in the loss of moral and spiritual illumination. We are responsible for "the light of the body" which is "the eye"—whether it be "single," or whether it be "evil."

We are to apply this to the circumstances in which we stand, to ourselves as immortal, and as destined to an immortality beyond the stars. What a wide meaning there is for each and every one of us, what a stirring personal appeal, in those words, "Hold that fast which thou hast, that no man take thy crown!"

May 5th, 1872.

Ascension Day.

THE HISTORICAL SIGNIFICANCE OF THE FORTY DAYS.

Acts i. 9.

"*And when He had spoken these things, while they beheld, he was taken up; and a cloud received him out of their sight.*"

AFTER His resurrection from the dead, our Saviour remained here on earth during a period of forty days. This was an interimistic period between His previous life on earth and His final glorification with the Father. The full meaning and significance of this remarkable period, we, of course, in our present circumstances are utterly unable to understand. Much here is a mystery for our faith, which, it were vain to attempt to explain or to make clear for the reason. Yet in the onward movement of our Saviour's mediatorial work, this period was one of the very highest significance, and it contains much that we may understand and much that is of importance for us to understand.

Our Saviour remained on the earth forty days after His resurrection and before his ascension. Why? Why did He not ascend to the right hand of the Father at once and immediately after His resurrection? We might also ask, Why did He not arise from the dead immediately instead of lying in the tomb for three days? He might have arisen in three hours, or in three moments just as well. Why did He not do so? Because such an immediate and instantaneous resurrection would have partaken too much of the nature of magic. It would have violated the natural historical sense of mankind. It would have been so far above and beyond human nature as to render it impossible to be grasped, and would not have stood forth so truly as an object for faith as it does.

Our Saviour's death was a real death, His burial a real burial. His lying in the tomb was a reality, and His resurrection also was a real historical fact about which there could be no doubt. There was no magic in His resurrection, as there might at least have seemed to be had He risen immediately after His burial.

So too with this interimistic period between His resurrection and His ascension. It was the necessary historic connection between our Saviour's previous life on earth, and His glorification at the right hand of the Father; and in this consists its main significance. It was a period of transition, during which, as we may suppose, our Saviour was gradually laying aside or throwing off His previous form of existence for one that was higher; though in what way this was done we, of course, do not at all know.

It was a period of transition from one form of existence to another, a bridging over of the chasm between the natural and the supernatural, the human and the divine, the finite and the infinite. This we may see from the fact that during this period our Saviour was the same person as before, and yet in many important regards His person during this period appears to have been widely different from what it had been previously. He was the same person, so we are expressly told in many passages relating His appearance to the disciples, as for instance to the two disciples on the way to Emmaus, and again in the upper chamber where Thomas was convinced of His identity. And yet, at the same time, a vast change had now passed upon Him. When He rose from the dead, it was not to return to the same kind of existence He had led previously. His resurrection in this regard was quite different from that of Lazarus, for example, who after having been raised from the dead, returned to precisely the same kind of life he had formerly led. Not so here, however. That kind of existence upon which our Saviour had now entered was far different, evidently, from our ordinary human life. This is sufficiently indicated by the fact of His sudden appearance and disappearance, as on the way to Emmaus, where after the interview in the home of the disciples, " He vanished out of their sight." He was no longer subject, as He had before been, to the limitations of time and space, although He was the same person precisely as when He was offered on the cross.

We can easily see in this way, then, that these forty days consisted a period of transition from one form of existence to another; and this period is of vast account and great significance as showing the historical character of Christianity. It shows very significantly that Christianity, originating in the person of Christ, is not a doctrine, but an ever on-flowing, organic life, in which no fact can be of a fragmentary nature, or occupy an isolated position.

We may suppose, too, that this period was of significance for the disciples themselves. During this period, no doubt, our Saviour had a great work to perform in reference to them in the way of instruction. He doubtless told them many things, not recorded in the Scripture, and gave them important directions and instructions concerning the government of the primitive Church. But their preparation for their sacred Apostolic office consisted not so much in such instruction in doctrine, or in such directions as to the management of the Church, as in His most solemn induction of them into their holy office, and the investing of them with its sacred obligations. As to the full meaning of all that had happened and was still further to happen in the institution of the Church, they must of course have been considerably in the dark; and it was not until the day of Pentecost that they came to a full and clear understanding of their divine commission.

To an earnest and reflecting mind no stronger proof of the authenticity of the Scriptures or the genuineness of the Gospel narrative, could possibly be given than the account of our Saviour's appearance on earth after His resurrection. That a Saviour, or a founder of a religious system, should be introduced or brought upon the stage shortly after He had been buried out of sight of men, when the world imagined that He was no more, was entirely beyond the conception of any mortal man, beyond all art and all thought. Men might indeed have conceived the idea of bringing the founder of a religion on the stage after he was dead, in the form of a pure spirit, but none ever would have dreamed of so presenting him as our Lord is represented by the Evangelists as having appeared during this period of forty days.

The appearance of our Saviour here on earth during this time was the natural preparation for His glorious ascension to the right hand of the Father, which was another step or stage in the great unfolding mystery of redemption. We see at once the close relation of the two. Had He ascended on high immediately after His resurrection, His ascension could never have been for us the same object of faith as it is now; for in such a case we might, and very probably would, have been in danger of regarding Him as ascending on high as a pure spirit, and not as taking with Him, in a glorified form, our human nature, as we know He did.

The ascension of our Saviour, however, stands related historically not only to all that went before, but to all that was to come after, not only to His resurrection from the dead, but also to His coming again to judge the quick and the dead.

For, when He ascended up on high, "Behold two men stood by them in white apparel which said, Ye men of Galilee, why stand ye gazing up unto heaven? This same Jesus which is taken up from you into heaven shall so come in like manner as ye have seen Him go into heaven"—reproving the disciples, as it were, for supposing that this was to be the end of the glorious work of redemption, chiding them for "gazing up into heaven," as if the Saviour were now gone into the heaven forever. "This same Jesus shall come again." Here was to be the final completion of the glorious work of Christ, His second coming. Toward this, all the different acts and successive stages of His life had been looking forward, and this is the one great problem of the world—the grand consummation toward which all things are now moving.

May 6, 1869. NOTE.—This sermon was written from memory after the delivery, and not from notes taken at the time.

The Fourteenth Sunday after Trinity.

OBEDIENCE THE WAY TO A KNOWLEDGE OF THE TRUTH.

John vii. 17.

"If any man will do his will, he shall know of the doctrine, whether it be of God, or whether I speak of myself."

REASON is the dignity and glory of our human life. By this we are distinguished from the animal world, in which instinct prevails. Reason, however, is not to be regarded as a simple or single power or faculty of the soul of man. On the contrary, it cannot be rightly contemplated except as being complex in its very nature, and as involving an entire order, or series, of powers or faculties wherein the intelligent nature of man is manifested.

There is, first of all, the intelligence, or the theoretical side of the reason, which is a power of taking in knowledge from the outside world, and which covers our intellectual life from the lowest and most primary forms of sensation up to what is sometimes called "Pure Thinking."

Then, secondly, we have the practical side of the reason—the will; the power of acting from within outward; of telling back on the things around us. The will is a part of the reason of man—for the will always implies an intelligible end or purpose of the act.

These two sides of the reason cannot be separated in actual fact, however much we may distinguish between the two for the purposes of our thinking and scientific reflection. For how can a man take any knowledge of outward things unless he first of all wills so to do? Or, how can a man will to do anything unless he has, at the same time, a knowledge of the thing he proposes to do? Yet it has ever been a vexed question with men of science to know which of these two, the theoretical or the practical side of the reason, is to be regarded as primary. Is the will in order to the intelligence, or the intelligence in order to the will?

Here in religion we meet the same psychological problem. It has always been a question whether of these two sides of the reason of man shall have the priority and the supremacy. Does religion begin in the form of light, or in the form of affection and love? It is a most important question indeed—a question of far-reaching significance, and of controlling influence for our theological thinking, and also for the interests of our practical Christian life and conduct.

In the light of the text, as well also as in the light of the best mental science, the priority belongs to the will, although men in every age are somehow, and singularly enough, ever prone to make far more account of the other side, viz., of the intelligence. It is not in the intelligence that the highest dignity of man consists, nor is it in the intelligence that the full power and majesty of the reason of man appear. It is in the will. There is no fact with which we need to be better acquainted than this; for there is none of greater importance for the proper understanding of our own wonderful constitution.

The will is the fundamental power everywhere. It is so in the divine mind, or in the constitution of the divine being. We must conceive of these two sides of the reason as existing in the constitution of the Godhead; but the passive side (intelligence) does not go before the active (the will). The being of God is the product of His own free activity. This is an unfathomable mystery, of course, which we cannot at all comprehend; but this at least we can plainly see, that God was not brought into existence by any causation beyond Himself. He comes by His own activity. He is self-created. In theology this has sometimes been called His *aseity*. Then, too, we cannot conceive of God having been thus brought to pass and then merely continuing to exist without the continued exercise of His own will. God cannot exist passively. His will is fundamental for His being.

What is thus seen to be true of the divine mind absolutely is also true of the created mind relatively. The activity of the will is the first and chief manifestation of the reason. Man becomes self-conscious in infancy by the power of his will. And this mysterious process we repeat every morning of our lives, when by the power of the will we awake out of our sleep. This is, of course, unfathomable. We cannot bring it within the scope of our science; but undoubtedly awakening takes place by a positive act of self-affirmation on the part of the mind. This is but one illustration amongst many that might be given to show how that reason first manifests itself in an act of the will.

The individual will, however, is not a law unto itself, but is bound evermore and always by a wider will existing beyond itself. The will encounters the law, and without the law the will is false. The relation between the two, however, is not mechanical, but free. Only when the law is freely embraced and affirmed by the created intelligence, can there be any entrance for the spirit of man into the sphere of freedom. It is on this ground that the freedom and power of the will depend—on being in full harmony with the divine will; and it is in view of this fundamental law of our being that the declaration of Christ, as given in the text, holds good.

That declaration stands in a peculiar connection. The Jews believed Him unlettered, because He had never learned. "How knoweth this man letters, having never learned?" But Jesus in the temple, and in the midst of the feast, confronts them and says, " My doctrine is not mine but His that sent me. If any man will do His will"—or, as it may be more properly rendered, "if any man wills, or is willing to do His will, he shall know of the doctrine, whether it be of God, or whether I speak of myself."

It is one of the most profound declarations of the New Testament. For it implies the absolute and unequivocal possession of the divine nature by Jesus Christ, the proof of which fact depends not (as I have often said) on separate texts or passages of Scripture, but is to be found rather in the abiding, perpetual consciousness as again and again expressed by our Saviour, that His will and His thinking were one with the will and the thinking of God. So was He one with the Father. This is an overwhelming proof. The evidence for the divinity of Christ commonly adduced from proof-texts of Scripture, as they are called, must in the end derive all its force and significance from this, "My doctrine is not mine, but His that sent me." Here is a clear consciousness of absolute identification with the divine mind. Let us now notice certain points in this simple test in the apprehension of religious truth, "If any man wills to do his will, he shall know of the doctrine."

It is a test that can be applied to the acquisition of all knowledge whatsoever, as we have already to some extent seen. The will leads the way in the apprehension of all truth. Yet men have a specious and plausible way of talking about the acceptance of the truths of the Gospel as if these could be embraced quite apart from the moral side of the question altogether. There are those who question the supernatural character of Christ, and say that the authority of the Gospel can get along very well without that. They appeal to the Sermon on the Mount as being the highest form of spiritual or religious truth; and they tell us that if we are only somehow persuaded that the body of all truth is to be found there, that is all that is necessary, without even considering the one great question which lies far back of that—this, namely, whether Christ was of divine origin or not. This is the leading article in the creed of rationalism. The theoretical side of the reason is violently divorced from the practical. In opposition to this specious belief we say that such a theory is contradicted by the actual fact of our own mental constitution, properly considered, as it certainly is by this most profound and far-reaching declaration of our Saviour's—"If any man wills to do His will, he shall know of the doctrine."

Another false conception lies somewhat in the opposite direction. The practical side of the reason may be divorced from the theoretical. There may be the form of doing God's will without the substance. The imagination of some is that all is well if we have reason to think that our life and conduct are right, no matter what our creed may be. But our Saviour here says that there must be something more than mere doing. The word "will," here, is not the auxiliary; it is the principal and the most emphatic word in the text. "If any man wills," is willing, and remains abidingly willing, "he shall know." The willing here lies back of the doing, being the fixed habit of the soul, and involving the consent of the whole man. This with the Saviour was the criterion.

The knowing comes by the willing. The reigning habit of the mind or the soul, in reference to the divine mind or will, is the one consideration of chief account in the apprehension of divine truth. This grand thought our Saviour presents for our consideration over and over again, as for example, when He says, "If thine eye be single"—that is, if the inward habit and disposition of the soul be right—"thy whole body shall be full of light." "But if the light that is in thee"—that is, if the inward, reigning spirit be not in accordance with the divine will—"be darkness, how great is that darkness." If the will be led away from the divine will, how can there be light? If the eye of the body refuse to see, or be turned away from the light of the natural sun in the heavens, how can there be light? "I am the light of the world: he that followeth me shall not walk in darkness, but shall have the light of life." So, too, in the interview with Nicodemus: "This is the condemnation that light is come into the world, and men loved darkness rather than light, because their deeds were evil. For every one that doeth evil"—that is, the habit of whose soul is to do evil—"hateth the light. But he that doeth truth"—here again it is "doing," indicating a settled determination or a fixed purpose of the mind and heart—"cometh to the light that his deeds may be made manifest that they are wrought in God."

We close with a few brief, practical reflections.

I. The single eye, then, is all in all. To have our will fixed on God, and on the doing of His will, as the reigning habit of the mind, this is a matter of the highest possible moment with us all.

II. But, there is a drawing here. "No man cometh unto the Father but by me," and "no man cometh to me except the Father draw him." We see how our will has been blinded and enfeebled by the fall. And we see also what a vain imagination is that which claims that nothing but education and culture are needful for a man, trusting in this way to work out the problem of our human life. There is no imagination in the mind or heart of man more fundamentally false than this. It matters not how much culture there may be from the cradle to the grave, it never can save men. And yet this miserable falsehood, which enters so largely into much of the education, culture and humanitarianism of this age generally, is the boasted claim of many to recognition and influence. We meet here a wonderful, though a sad illustration of that blindness in the understanding which has been superinduced by the fall. Reason left to itself, and to the operation of its own laws, never can lead toward the divine will; it is forever leading away from it.

From all this we find that the only remedy for the ills under which our common humanity is suffering is to be found not at all within the range of its own powers. The help must always come from a higher source. If any man wills to do God's will he shall know of the doctrine.

September 10, 1871.

The Nineteenth Sunday after Trinity.

THE KNOWLEDGE OF GOD THROUGH CHRIST ALONE.

Matthew xi. 27.

"*All things are delivered unto me of my Father; and no man knoweth the Son but the Father; neither knoweth any man the Father save the Son, and he to whomsoever the Son will reveal him.*"

THE perfection of man's being consists in the perfect development of his religious nature, and the great aim of all revelation is to bring man to a knowledge of God through Jesus Christ His Son. Such a knowledge of God, is, in one view, rendered necessary by the demands of our own constitution or nature. There is in man a three-fold form of consciousness—a consciousness of self, of the world, and of God. In the very conception or idea of self-consciousness there is a necessity for consciousness of that which is not self—the outside, external world; and the consciousness of that which is not ourselves is quite as original and necessary as the consciousness of that which is. But alongside of this necessarily involved consciousness of the external world, there is in every soul an equally necessary and original consciousness of God. Man has an instinctive sense of absolute existence—of an existence, or a Being, above and beyond himself and above and beyond the world. Were this wanting in the original constitution of the soul, no amount of external evidence could bring any man to a sense of such an absolute existence. After all that may be said upon the subject, and when all the arguments men have invented to establish the existence of a God, the great, fundamental, immovable and unanswerable argument for God's being will be found to consist in this original God-consciousness in us. This sense of God is universal, all men have it, heathen as well as Christian. On the part of heathenism it is a negative evidence for the truth of Christianity; but of itself it is quite insufficient for the purpose of man's perfection; as we can see when we consider that the ancient heathen world, though in full possession of this sense of the absolute, yet was led further and further into all forms of error, at one time into the deification of nature, at another into a deification of human beings.

The mere sense, or consciousness, of the absolute is not enough, therefore, to bring us to a knowledge of God. We need an exemplification or manifestation of the absolute in some outward form, in order that our consciousness of the absolute may assume a form commensurate with the character of the object. Such a manifestation we do indeed meet in the natural world, as the Psalmist says, "The heavens declare the glory of God, and the firmament sheweth his handy-work;" but such a revelation, whether in external nature, or in our own physical and moral constitution, or in the world of history, is but partial and relative, and falls immeasurably short of what is necessary to a full knowledge of God.

Our Saviour, in the language of our text, challenges our homage to His own person as the only full and perfect manifestation of the being of God. It was in view of the fact that not many wise, mighty or learned men had comprehended this full manifestation of the being of God, and that the simple-minded fishermen-disciples, and others in the humble walks of life had apprehended Him with a true faith, that He was moved to exclaim, " I thank thee, O Father, Lord of heaven and earth, that thou hast hid these things from the wise and prudent, and hast revealed them unto babes and sucklings. Even so, Father, for so it seemed good in thy sight." And then, as if to show the fulness of His own person, as the perfect manifestation of God, He adds, " All things are delivered unto me of my Father . . . neither knoweth any man the Father save the Son, and he to whomsoever the Son will reveal him."

Observe here how the person of Christ is made to stand over against every other revelation of God. "No man knoweth the Father save the Son,"—no man ever has known, no man ever can know the Father, in any other way. All other revelation, without this, is of no avail. Men talk of "looking through nature up to nature's God"—but Christ says, " No man knoweth the Father but the Son, and he to whomsoever the Son will reveal him."

Observe further that there seems to be implied or suggested here some sort or degree of inferiority on the part of the Son to the Father, the reference being to the historical manifestation of the Son in His state of earthly humiliation. But it is also to be particularly observed in this passage, as well as in others of similar import, that a relation between the Father and the Son is implied as existing in the very constitution of the Godhead itself, and prior to all time and human history. The very idea of the Father having delivered all things to the Son, in order that He might be a perfect representation of the Father, implies a previous relation between the two. The Father could never thus have delivered all things to one not His equal. The mere idea of God's having delivered all things in this way to Moses, for example, or to Abraham, or even to the angel Gabriel, in such way that they might say that their knowledge was identical with that of God, is blasphemous. In every passage in which Christ claims full knowledge of the Father, He also claims a full and perfect identity with Him. There is no force in the argument drawn from the New Testament against the absolute divinity of Christ. There could be no delegation of such high power and majesty to any creature, no matter how high his position may have been. When Christ says, "All things are delivered unto me of my Father," it is to say "I have full capacity to be like God, to be equal with Him." Here is a claim of co-equal existence with the Father. Here is the eternal generation of the Son. By this only was it possible for Christ to be our Mediator, to stand between heaven and earth, God and man. "All things are mine," He says. The will the power, the attributes of God passed over into His person as Christ Jesus. It was only in virtue of this relation that Christ could at all stand among men as their deliverer.

Only deity can be capacious of deity. "As the Father hath life in himself, so hath he given to the Son to have life in himself." The Son is never in the New Testament represented as inferior to the Father. He is "the brightness of God's glory, and the express image of his person," and as such He became incarnate as the highest revelation of God to man. This is the whole sense of the Gospel. The Gospel goes far beyond all other religions, none of which has power really to bring God and man together any nearer than in that comparatively poor and inadequate revelation in the world of nature to which we have referred. The presence of God in His Son stands unmeasurably above His presence in the world of nature. Christ says, "I am the way, the truth and the life. No man cometh unto the Father but by me." Oh what a depth of meaning in that declaration, "He that hath seen me hath seen the Father!" In the constitution of His own person, as the living connexion between heaven and earth, the highest form of humanity was taken up into indissoluble union with absolute divinity. It was deity enshrined in humanity; and Christ thus became, absolutely, "The Way"—the only way of approach to God, and in and through Him only could God be known. No one can know the Father save only he "to whomsoever the Son will reveal him."

The revelation spoken of here, however, is not one of doctrine merely. It is deeper than anything purely intellectual. It involves a common life and fellowship of existence. All knowledge of God is, fundamentally and in the depths of its origin, intuitional. It does not start with self-conscious reflection, but with an intuitional perception based upon a community of existence. Much that is supposed to be an apprehension of divine things falls far short of it. We cannot know God, as it were, at arms' length—by ratiocination. Such knowledge of God lowers Him to the position of a mere creature. God cannot at all be apprehended by such external thinking. So long as I think I am studying outside of deity, so that God shall be to me an object of knowledge, I am deceiving myself. God cannot be known in that way. There must be a union and communion with Him, first of all; and only when we are brought into direct union with Him who is the Truth, can we be in such fellowship with the Godhead that we may know God. In this way we can see something of the profound meaning of our Saviour's declaration, "No man knoweth the Father save the Son, and he to whomsoever the Son will reveal him."

This is the mystery of Christianity. And it was in view of the mystery here involved that our Lord exclaimed, "I thank thee, O Father, Lord of heaven and earth, that thou hast hid these things from the wise and prudent, and hast revealed them unto babes and sucklings;" because "these things" are beyond the grasp of the human mind, beyond the grasp of philosophy, and beyond the ken of those who rise to the sublimest heights in the wisdom of the world; and yet they may be and are revealed unto babes! As knowledge enters the mind of the babe, by virtue first of all of its living, organic relation to the world of humanity and to the world of nature, so there can be no true knowing of God except upon the basis of an antecedent communion with Him. And this simple way of knowing God is possible only in connection with the person of Christ.

We can now see how sublimely grand is the declaration that follows, and how naturally it springs out of what goes before—"Come unto me, all ye that labor and are heavy laden, and I will give you rest."—Ye that are perplexed in regard to the problem of your own existence, and have been dreaming concerning the future life, "Come unto me!" Nothing more sublime than this can be conceived of. It is an overwhelming argument. "Come unto me"—unto the person of Christ; not to His doctrines, His commands or His example, but to Himself. This is the end of our existence, the key to its proper understanding—to bring us forth from the dark prison house of our fallen nature into the light and freedom presented in Christ Jesus, the hope of immortality.

September 5, 1869.

The Twentieth Sunday after Trinity.

THE GOSPEL FOR THE POOR.

Luke vii. 22.

" To the poor the Gospel is preached."

THE immediate occasion for this declaration of our Lord was the visit of the disciples of John the Baptist, who had, it would seem, come to stand in some doubt as to His mission. The significant inquiry, "Art thou he that should come? or look we for another?" was of the nature of a most serious and solemn challenge of the ministry of Jesus; and the equally remarkable reply to the inquiry was designed to afford the greatest assurance, not only to the disciples of John, but also to all subsequent ages: "Go your way, and tell John what things ye have seen and heard; how the blind see, the lame walk, the lepers are cleansed, the deaf hear, the dead are raised, to the poor the gospel is preached."

Poverty, in the general sense of the term, signifies a state of want, wretchedness and misery. The poor may be considered as lacking the outward conveniences or necessities of life; but this outward poverty is only a figure of one that is more far-reaching and more profound; such as the loss of the senses, sickness, trial, bereavement and death, all the consequence of sin. And a powerful argument for the truth of the Gospel lies in the very significant fact that it alone presents a sufficient remedy and cure for poverty in the widest sense of the word. It is indeed "Glad Tidings" to the poor, and it is preached with efficacy just in the proportion that they are poor to whom it is preached. The divine origin and power of the Gospel are manifested in this striking fact. The general proposition laid down in the text may be established by three or four considerations:

I. The Gospel is a divine message which is designed to reach even to the poor, and to offer them the only truly radical cure of their poverty. It is a Gospel to the poor; not to the rich, or the healthy, or the high, or the great and noble among men. If it were addressed to any of these, it would not be radical enough to reach the true origin of the evils from which our humanity suffers.

In this regard the Gospel presents a most striking contrast with the various schemes which men have devised, from time to time in the course of history, for the alleviation of the sufferings of humanity. Such schemes originate sometimes in the political world, sometimes in the philosophical; or it may be some educational or social device; and each scheme of philanthropy is thought, for the time at least, to be all that is needed to set the world right. But the great difficulty with all these is that they are not radical enough. They may be good and do good in one portion of the community, but they do not reach to the ground of the evil. The philosophy of the ancients was only for the upper classes, the great masses of the people not being reached by it, except in the most general and indirect way. It reached, even at its best estate, only those evils which were superficial.

Now, over against all these schemes, the Gospel is "Glad Tidings" to the poor (who constitute the great body of the race in every age) and not to the rich. It would amount to but very little if the upper classes of society were to be set right while the masses were left in their misery. The Gospel reaches down into the deep and dark abyss of human sin and suffering, even to its remotest recesses, because it is deeper, more radical than any other cure for human woe that has ever been devised, carrying with it the force of a divine origin. Nothing else can reach so deep. The Gospel says, "Except a man be born of water and the Spirit, he cannot enter into the Kingdom of God." It proposes itself as the power of a new creation as radical as life itself, reaching even to the regeneration of the world at large. The more the Gospel of Christ is considered, in all its simplicity, the more it is seen to include a power adapted to the necessities of the race, and the more its divine origin appears in this very fact.

II. An argument for the divine character of the Gospel appears when we consider its true catholicity or universality, whereby it is adapted to our humanity considered as a universality. What takes hold of the universal must itself be universal. Hence all these schemes which we have just now alluded to are eclectic, as the term now is, and cannot be universal or catholic. It was but what was to be expected that the greater part of the race could not come within the scope of the ancient schemes. All that philosophy could do was to reach the better classes of minds, which included a comparatively very small number of men. So all educational and political schemes reach only a small portion of the human family. Before the time of Christ, politics concerned itself with the culture of patriotism, valor or philanthropy. These were the great virtues. All men outside of this estate of human culture were of a different caste, castaways, barbarians. All that the ancient civilization attempted was to reach a certain class.

Now, in direct contrast with this, the Gospel is constitutionally catholic, universal. The millions and hundreds of millions in heathen lands, and the millions of human beings that are the dregs of society in Christian countries; these constitute " the poor," and to these the Gospel is addressed. " Go ye into all the world, and preach the Gospel to every creature." " God sent not His Son into the world to condemn the world, but that the world through him might be saved." These, and many similar declarations show the adaptation of the Gospel to the race considered as a whole. It does not propose a salvation ending in a philosophy for the study of a few, nor the merely social well-being of certain classes, nor even a bare dream of social improvement by which matter shall subserve the purposes of mind and, as some think, by which the millenium shall be ushered in. The Gospel makes no account of these. " By one man sin entered into the world, and death by sin." The curse is universal. It reaches down to the very foundations of society, and if it is ever to be removed at all, the remedy proposed must be commensurate with the malady. We cannot help but see that the Gospel goes to the bottom of the curse. It is indeed objected by some that the Gospel does not include secular objects and pursuits, and that it regards these as accidental and secondary. Humanitarianism does not recognize the Gospel because it does not seem to make enough account of the outward well-being of men. That is no proper objection, however, but only an argument for the divine character of the Gospel; for, while the Gospel does not *directly* address itself to the amelioration of these evils (as it undoubtedly would were it of human origin) it does reach them indirectly, and is designed to cure them most effectually, by going down to that which is more general, and in which they are all included, the secret source of all the evils of our humanity.

III. The argument acquires additional force when we consider the adaptation of the Gospel to the wants of the poor to whom it is addressed. It claims to be the sovereign remedy for the ills from which they suffer, and in every age they have been disposed to welcome it. If the philosophy of Plato or that of Hegel were presented to them, they could not at all understand it. But they have a capacity for comprehending the Gospel, which is instinctively recognized as being what they need. They at once see this, feel it, know it; and this remarkable adaptation of the Gospel to the wants of the poor, and the instinctive recognition of the Gospel by the poor as being what they need, affords a most powerful argument for the divine origin of the Gospel. We need not develop at length this remarkable adaptation. The Gospel alone delivers from an evil conscience, gives joy and hope to the poor, in comparison with which all other remedial schemes are naught. It presents its claims boldly, and with full assurance promises rest and peace to the troubled soul. Its language in every age, to the oppressed, the despised, the poor, is: "Come unto me, and I will give you rest." "I am come, not to call the righteous, but sinners to repentance." "They that are whole need not a physician, but they that are sick." The Gospel offers itself to those laboring under a sense of poverty, both as regards this world and that which is to come; and, as it is suited to their wants, so also are they found in every age gladly to respond to its challenge, so far as their power to apprehend it may go.

It is a striking picture which is here presented. On

the one side there is a grand scheme, such as angels desire to look into, wrought out for the human family by Christ; on the other side a whole race, groaning and heavy-laden. And so soon as these two are brought together, they are at once found to be reciprocal, and mutually complemental. Men find the only complement of their poverty in the Gospel of Christ, and this is, indeed, a grand argument for its divine character. And this is the argument which the poor need. Ninety-nine persons out of every one hundred need no other proof of the Gospel than their own experience. Where the case is so universal, how can it be established by any proof beyond itself? This is true in the experience of all of us. The divine character of Christ rests upon this same argument. He cannot be proved by anything outside of Himself. He is His own proof to the soul. And so, the Gospel being fundamentally adapted to the true needs of mankind, it sets the poor in new relations to God, giving them power to live in obedience to God's commands, and to cry, "Abba, Father." The argument culminates in the success of the Gospel, as seen in the history of Christianity. All other religions, all other schemes, whether of philosophy or government, have failed to present a sufficient remedy. Nothing can ever be accomplished by all the power of science. Though all the powers of the natural world be mastered, to what would it all amount for the cure of the radical misery of our fallen life?

In conclusion, all poverty, though undoubtedly an evil, is nevertheless a means of grace, when properly considered. It cannot fail, when rightly used, to subserve the salvation of the soul. And this is an important reflection for us all. Poverty, as a mere outward privation, even, is a means of grace. We may abuse the sacrament, yet the sacrament carries power in itself, nevertheless. So with poverty. It is often called a curse, when men are dissatisfied with the allotments of life ; but in the light of the Gospel it is a means of grace, a blessing in disguise. It offers to men the occasion of coming near to Christ, an occasion which they could not otherwise have. Without faith it is a curse; but so soon as men see that there is in it a power of bringing them to a reconciliation with the Heavenly Father, and of making them submissive to His will, they must recognize it not as a curse, but as a blessing. Poverty, in one form or another, is sent from God, who may indeed also send health and strength and riches, which are likewise means of grace to all who rightly receive and employ these advantages. But all men, in coming to Christ, must be poor ; if not with an outward poverty, then with an inward. Otherwise they cannot possess the kingdom ; for our Saviour says, " Blessed are the poor in spirit, for theirs is the kingdom of heaven."

September 12, 1869.

The Twentieth Sunday after Trinity.

CHRIST THE ONLY SATISFYING PORTION OF THE SOUL.

Matthew xi. 28-30.

"*Come unto me, all ye that labor and are heavy laden, and I will give you rest. Take my yoke upon you, and learn of me; for I am meek and lowly in heart; and ye shall find rest unto your souls. For my yoke is easy, and my burden is light.*"

THESE words may be taken as an invitation addressed directly to all such as have become awakened to the fact of their sinfulness and are looking about them for help and relief. Here they are required to look away from themselves, and are challenged to fasten on Jesus Christ as the only source of righteousness and salvation.

In a wider view the text may be regarded as calling on all those who suffer in body, mind or outward estate, to look to the Lord Jesus as the one great source of all security and peace.

It is not necessary, however, to restrict or limit this passage to either the one or the other class. The passage contemplates our fallen life in its widest view. Whether men are aware of it or not, the condition in which we all are by nature is one of poverty and want, from which men are, in spite of themselves, impelled to seek for deliverance. Our life cannot but be regarded as one of toil, labor, conflict, whether it be prosecuted in righteousness or in sin. In our natural life there is no rest or peace to the human spirit, and it is in view of this our natural state, that our Saviour here appeals not only to all those who heard Him utter these words, but to all succeeding generations down to the end of time, "Come unto me, all ye that labor, and are heavy-laden, and I will give you rest."

We cannot possibly conceive of a more grand and majestic position than that which our Saviour here assumes, as over against the world of nature and history. There is no meaning in the language except as implying that the true sense of the world is comprehended in His own person, in such a way that He has a right to place Himself over against the world and challenge the obedience and homage of men in opposition to all other attractions whatsoever. "Come unto me," as over against the world at large, as over against trial and affliction, as over against pleasure and sensuality, as over against literature, art and science, "Come unto me," all ye that labor in other directions and seek rest from other sources, "and I will give you rest."

Looking at the language of the text in this way, we see at once that it involves an absolutely overwhelming argument for our Saviour's divinity. The language is that of a person possessing a full, conscious superiority to the whole world. There is a powerful argument here (for all those who have the power or disposition to apprehend its significance) for the absolute Truth as being embodied in the person of Christ. Our Saviour could never have been in the calm possession of this conscious superiority to the whole world, under its widest view, unless He was what He claimed to be—the full revelation, the absolute utterance of the most high God.

For no one feels that language such as this ill-befits the Saviour's lips. We do not feel that it is too high or pretentious. Such language in the lips of any other man in all the world would be felt at once to be blasphemy. But, as spoken by Christ, this language approves itself to the deepest moral feeling of the world in every age. And we have here, therefore, a proof of His divinity far beyond that afforded by His miracles or the fulfilled prophecies, the one great and convincing evidence of His divinity proceeding here as always from His own person.

It is only natural that He should have thus spoken, as we can see readily enough when we consider the connection in which these words were uttered. He had been speaking of the privileges of the cities of the plain, and denouncing their sin in not having recognized the day of their visitation. Immediately upon this follow the words, " At that time Jesus answered and said, I thank thee O Father, Lord of heaven and earth, that thou hast hid these things from the wise and prudent and hast revealed them unto babes. Even so, Father; for so it seemed good in thy sight. All things are delivered unto me of my Father: and no man knoweth the Son but the Father: neither knoweth any man the Father, save the Son, and he to whomsoever the Son will reveal him." With what overwhelming force does not the text follow upon these marvelous words! "All things are delivered unto me of my Father "—it would not be at all possible to deliver these things to a mere creature. He to whom they are delivered must be of a nature fully commensurate with His by whom they are given. In a word, our Saviour here claims to be absolutely co-equal with the Father: and it is just in view of this co-equality and the immense superiority to the whole world as involved in that co-equality, that He exclaims with such infinite significance, "Come unto me and I will give you rest."

How is it, now, that men are required to come to Christ? What is meant by coming to Christ? Undoubtedly the reference here is to faith. The exercise of faith is an act by which we come to Christ. But this act of faith involves certain steps or stages.

I. It involves, first of all, a consideration of what we are, and what the world around us is. So long as men are not brought to consider seriously their circumstances as they actually are, they cannot be brought to comprehend their miseries, either in a natural or a spiritual sense. "They that are whole need not a physician, but they that are sick." But a consciousness of spiritual sickness requires a self-knowledge, as well as an apprehension also of the fleeting and evanescent character of the world around us. And not only is the whole world vain, but our own being is also vain, under its merely natural view, and even also in its spiritual character, when this is considered by itself. The more we come to understand ourselves in this light, the more we come to stand aghast at our own nature as something horrible and hollow. For we are a world of delusion, disorder and darkness, without light and without hope.

II. All this involves a conviction of sin. This conviction must go so far with us as to amount to an overwhelming persuasion. In these circumstances, then, we are prepared to turn away from the world to Christ. And this is our second point. The call from Christ, in the invitation of the text, is "Come away from all this misery and woe to Me." Turning implies a movement away from something and a movement toward something. The first step in the turning, here, is the conviction of which we have been speaking. Then comes the actual turning—this is the second stage: and yet the two are never separated in actual fact, because it is only by the growing apprehension of what Christ is that we come at all to understand what our sin and misery is. In proportion as we come to apprehend the fulness of life in Him, in that proportion precisely do we come to understand the vanity and misery of our earthly state.

It is in this act of turning that the act of faith appears. Here there must be a continuous turning from and a turning to. In the words of our catechism, there must be "a dying of the old man and a quickening of the new man." Yet these two do not stand apart from each other. They are in reality mutually complemental and necessary, being opposite sides of the same act. There is no turning from the world except we receive Christ into the affections. The two sides of faith, here, form a single act. The positive side lies with Christ, the negative with the world. There is no true negation of the world that does not arise from the power of a higher principle.

Hence men have never truly succeeded in renouncing and forsaking the world by any schemes of philosophy. Hence, also, the law as given in the hands of Moses was not sufficient to lead men to a true and lasting rest and peace. There is needed for this purpose an actual coming down of the Godhead into our humanity, in order that our humanity may be lifted up above the vanity in which its life is ever flowing. And this coming into our humanity must be personal on the part of God, so that in turning away from themselves and the world, men are challenged to turn to the actual person of the Son of God. We are to come to Him; not to His words, or His doctrine, but to Himself. And this we are to do continually, in the way of faith. All can come, as all are invited to come—high and low, rich and poor, old and young. Even little children can do this.

III. The third fact to which we invite attention is some consideration of the office performed by the means of grace in this coming to Christ. The movement of the soul toward Christ, here, is of course spiritual throughout, holding in the region of the spirit of man. But faith is not a mere abstraction. Christianity is something historical and not magical. It reaches down into the actual world in which we live: and faith involves not only an inward but also an outward act in reference to the person of Christ. Provision is made for this in the Church by the means of grace, which are media by which our faith is led to high spiritual results. The act of coming to Christ is not completed except by the believing use of these means. It is in vain to believe in a power to save unless we also make due and proper account of the means by which this salvation is to become real to us, instead of being a mere ghostly abstraction. "Come unto me" implies outward means of coming as well as an inward disposition to come. Many make use of the outward side without any spiritual profit, because the means of grace are made use of in a merely outward and mechanical way. Nevertheless it is an error on the other side to say that these means are of no account. We are undoubtedly to use means, must use means, if Christianity is to be anything more to us than a mere Gnostic abstraction; but with these means we are to have such an inward spiritual apprehension of Christ through the Holy Ghost as shall make them truly effectual for their high ends and purposes. "If any man have not the spirit of Christ, he is none of His." This entering into the Spirit of Christ is what constitutes an effectual coming to Him, and it is only in this way that the promised rest can be received. We must have the spirit, the mind of Christ—the spirit of self-denial and self-renunciation. " He that loseth his life for my sake shall find it." " Except a corn of wheat fall into the ground and die, it abideth alone." Thus are we to " learn" of Him, not of the world: we are to learn many a lesson which seems hard enough to the flesh, but the cheering word is " My yoke is easy and my burden is light."

Finally, Christ says in the way of a most glorious promise, "I will give you rest." Wherein consists this rest? It is begun in this life, but will be completed fully only in the life that is to come ; and it consists, first of all, in a sense of rightness in regard to God. Our life and happiness in this world (so far indeed as we can regard true happiness as attainable here) depend upon the harmonious working together of our entire organization, physical and spiritual, toward their own proper end and purpose. That is what we mean by health, in the widest sense of the word—a perfect harmony of the several parts of organic life. We know what health is, not so much by having it as by not having it; by passing through sickness and then recovering. In every sickness there is a crisis, a turning point. The passing of that crisis is an unspeakable blessing, for now the principle of order has again begun to prevail.

There is something like this in regard to the soul. Sin is a sickness in the soul, a lack of harmony, disorder, confusion, so that the soul of fallen man is like " the troubled sea when it cannot rest, whose waters cast up mire and dirt." Where the fundamental, constitutional law of a man's being is violated, how can there be rest or peace for him? His life is out of harmony with itself, being turned away from its ultimate end and purpose and fastened back upon itself.

Now, the very act of coming to Christ, though weak and feeble enough in the outstart, is a turning-point in the disease, a crisis in the great sin-sickness of the soul, a decision by which Christ is acknowledged and the world cast off and disowned: it is an act by which Christ becomes the loadstar of a man's existence. Though at first there is no perfect harmony in the soul when that step is taken, and all around still seems confusion and darkness, yet there springs up to such a man a light on the tempest-tossed sea of life, it may be away in the distance, yet still a star of hope rejoicing the soul. The confused life now begins to revolve, like the stars in their orbits, around the absolute Good and Right. The simple act of turning to Christ is itself at once somehow felt to be an act of rest and peace, a sense of returning health which no power on earth besides can give.

This sense of rightness in the soul is, at the same time, the beginning of an inward emancipation from the power of the world, an emancipation which cannot, in any manner whatsoever, be secured by any other power. Science, Art, Morality, Culture, Education—in a word all humanitarian efforts of whatsoever kind they be, no matter how high their claims may be, must most hopelessly and lamentably fail at last to give rest or peace to the troubled soul. And they who look for help in any of these directions are cheated at last as with the hollow mockery of a dream. It is with them "even as when a hungry man dreameth, and behold he eateth; but he awaketh, and his soul is empty: or as when a thirsty man dreameth, and behold he drinketh; but he awaketh, and behold he is faint."

At the same time, also, we need to bear in mind that the perfect rest of the soul which is involved in this coming to Christ cannot be attained in this world, but will be reached only in that world which is to come.

October 22, 1871.

The Twenty-third Sunday after Trinity.

SEARCHING THE SCRIPTURES.

John v. 39-40.

"*Search the Scriptures: for in them ye think ye have eternal life: and they are they which testify of me. And ye will not come to me, that ye might have life.*"

THESE words were addressed to the unbelieving Jews. Their lack of faith in the person of the Saviour was certainly not owing to a want of evidence. They had the testimony of John the Baptist, who was sent to them as a special witness of Christ. But they had even greater witness than this: for our Saviour says expressly that He had greater witness than that of John, viz., the works which He did: and the appeal which he here makes is to the self-evidencing power of His works. This evidence, as coming forth from His own person, far exceeded in weight and authority any witness that John could possibly have borne. The works of Christ bare witness that the Father had sent Him. The authentication here was not of an outward, external character, as was that of the descending dove. The evidence here is abiding and not temporary, addresses itself to the inward sense and not to the outward eye: and that which caused this authentication to fail of its object lay not with Christ, but with the unbelieving Jews themselves. "Ye have neither heard his voice at any time, nor seen his shape. And ye have not his word abiding in you." This was the true secret of their failure to receive Christ. Had there been an inward harmony between their minds and the divine mind, they would at once have acknowledged the claims of the Saviour. That they did not do so was a proof of the absence of all such harmony. Then follows the text.

It is commonly thought that the meaning of the text is that all who search the Scriptures will find the truth. But the Saviour here means to teach something quite different from this, viz., that unless first of all the mind of God be in him who reads the Scriptures, he will not find the truth. The Jews did search the Scriptures most diligently, and yet did not thereby attain to a knowledge of the truth. "Search the Scriptures"—or, as it should be more properly translated, "Ye do search the Scriptures"—"for in them ye think ye have eternal life: and they are they which testify of me." And yet, although these Jews, learned in the law, did most diligently search the Scriptures, and although these Scriptures did everywhere testify of Christ, yet when He appeared amongst them they did not recognize Him. Where was the fault? In their searching of the Scriptures, or in God manifest in the flesh?

There is no truth more important than this, that the study of the Scriptures depends on the disposition of the mind of the student. If the mind that seeks for the truth be not like "the single eye," of which the Saviour elsewhere speaks, then all will be darkness. The Scriptures may be studied in the interest of a false religion: there may be no sympathy with the absolute truth to begin with, and then the Scriptures will only be a savor of death unto death and not of life unto life. Of what account was it that these Jews did search the Scriptures, so long as there was in them no sympathy with the divine mind? They searched for the truth with no heart to obey the truth, or even to accept it, when found. "Ye will not come unto me that ye might have life." If they could not understand Him, they could not understand the Scriptures. The great difficulty was in their will. "If any man will—is willing to—do His will, he shall know of the doctrine." Without placing himself in a posture of preliminary subordination of the will to the mind of God, no man can ever attain to a knowledge of the truth.

The text implies that man has a want of life. We have physical, intellectual, moral life, but all this falls far short of the proper conception of life. Life, in the true sense, can come only from Christ, the fountain-source of all life. "Ye will not come to me that ye might have life." What the Jews expected was salvation by doctrines or laws; but what all men need is not doctrine or laws for the outward conduct, but life; and without this all doctrines and all laws are of little account.

Why is it that, in the days of our Saviour as also in our own, men will not come to Christ?

I. They have no sense of their misery and want. The want of such sense is the result of moral death, involving both moral and intellectual darkness. Such persons will not come to Christ because they have no lively sense of their want. "They that are whole need not a physician, but they that are sick."

II. Men may, to a certain extent be brought to feel their need, and yet be prone to believe that their disease need only be partially cured. When men first become sensible of their want of righteousness and the necessity of pardon, the first tendency of the mind is not toward Christ, because the cure to be found in Him is too radical, and does not at all agree with their great self-love. The mind is not ready for a complete self-renunciation. Such men become moral; submit themselves to doctrines and precepts, and hope to be saved. So long as any hope can be drawn from themselves in any way, men will not come to Christ.

III. The act of coming to Christ necessarily involves the most radical change that can possibly be wrought in a man's existence. "Except a man be born again he cannot see the kingdom of God." "If any man come to me, and hate not his father and mother . . . he cannot be my disciple." This is the very hardest service to which the human spirit can be put. Men will sacrifice property and submit to much personal inconvenience to establish a self-righteousness, but when the full claims of the Gospel come, and they are asked to forsake all to follow Christ, then comes the struggle. So also men may be powerfully awakened to their need of salvation, and yet fail of attaining to it. The human spirit can be made ready for such a renunciation only by the power of God.

In St. Luke's Gospel we are told that many would have followed Christ, but when He said, "Foxes have holes, and birds of the air have nests, but the Son of Man hath not where to lay his head," they hesitated. "Lord, suffer me first to go and bury my father," was the plea of one; but our Lord said, "Let the dead bury their dead," for this request to go and bury his father was only an excuse for a present, immediate renunciation of all in following the Saviour. Another said, "Lord, I will follow thee; but let me first go and bid them farewell which are at home at my house." But this also was an excuse for immediate obedience.

How full of significance, how truly expressive are not these simple passages! Among the other truths and lessons which they convey, we see this: that the person of our Lord is of infinitely greater weight and authority than all external argument or proof. His authority is self-authenticating. He is His own argument. May we ever be able to exclaim with the disciples, when our Lord asked them whether they too would go away from Him, "Lord, to whom shall we go? Thou hast the words of eternal life!"

October 3, 1869.

The Fourth Sunday before Advent.

THE UNBROKEN COMMUNION OF THE SAINTS.

The Gospel for the Day—St. Matthew ix. 18-26.

" While he spake these things unto them, behold there came a certain ruler, and worshipped him, saying, My daughter is even now dead; but come and lay thy hand upon her, and she shall live."

WE enter now upon the closing section of the Church Year. The Church Year, considered as a whole, may be regarded as falling into two grand divisions. In the first half of the Church Year we have presented for our consideration the leading objective facts of redemption, from the birth of our Lord to the coming of the Holy Ghost on the day of Pentecost. In the second half, which follows a somewhat parallel course, we have the subjective side as the leading theme, the Scripture lessons and the collects having chiefly in view the work of redemption as this is carried forward in the life and experience of the believer. These two orders are in a certain sense parallel, and yet under another view, the second is the reverse of the first. The first begins with the birth of Christ, and following the leading facts of His life and ministry, reaches its culmination in His ascension and glorification at the right hand of the Father, thus proceeding from the less to the more perfect, and following the course of the sun in the heavens at this season of the year. The second grand division of the Church Year, on the other hand, begins as it were above, and then in a steadily advancing process seems to come down, being a continual letting down of the higher into the lower life.

In that way the movement corresponds to the movement or progress of decay in our natural life which is ever fading, and growing older, and passing away. In this way, it might seem indeed as if the second half of the Church Year were in direct contrast with the first, if not indeed in conflict with it, but it is not so. One can easily see that the two are mutually complemental. The latter half of the Church Year in reality makes room for, and indeed by its very nature, demands the former; for it is only when old things are thus passing away that room can be made for all things to become new by the coming in of a new and higher life. The new life is thus ever advancing and growing while the old is receding and decaying. In the order of the Church Year we find something of a correspondence with the order of the natural year, in the outward visible world, in which after the season of the harvest, there is a continued and ever increasing decline and decay, all nature drawing in her energies and powers, in order to make room for the advent of the season of the spring.

We stand, now, in this latter half of this great season, having come nigh unto the end of the Church Year. At the same time also we are in the midst of the decline and fall of the great and mysterious world of nature. All colors, all sounds and objects at this season of the year conspire to remind us that all nature is doomed to perish, and that we too, as comprehended in the general system of nature, are passing away. We cannot help feeling that—cannot avoid that sense. The feeling enters into our poetry, and forces itself irresistibly upon the minds and hearts of men everywhere. It is felt by the uncultured as well as the refined and educated, by the heathen as well as by the Christian world. In harmony with this feeling arising from a contemplation of nature at this season of the year, that portion of the Church Year in which we presently stand is calculated very strikingly and forcibly to impress us with the same feeling, viz., that we are fading and passing away; but the Church Year here does for us what no contemplation of nature can ever accomplish—it opens the way for the incoming of a higher life.

In this way Christian experience, as something infinitely superior, rises above the merely pagan, natural feeling which men experience when they look on the world of nature and are sadly sensible that, beautiful and noble though it be, it is after all doomed to decay and is rapidly passing away. *We* look for "a new heaven and a new earth." We can see this strong, positive Christian sentiment prevailing in the Gospel and Epistle lessons, and especially in the collects employed at this season of the Church Year. We see it here, for example, in the Gospel for the day, in the case of the ruler's daughter, and in the healing of the woman having the issue of blood. This Gospel lesson is designed to bring home to us the feeling of Christ's superior power as contrasted with the poverty and frailty of nature within us and around us. Were there nothing to look to or to rely on other than this mere frame of nature around us, there could be no hope for a new and higher life beyond. Hence in the Gospel lesson for the day, the fading of the old life makes way for the coming of the new.

We have the same thought, also, in the Epistle lesson for the day, (Col. I. 9–14) "For this cause we also, since the day we heard it, do not cease to pray for you, and to desire that ye might be filled with the knowledge of his will, in all wisdom and spiritual understanding; that ye might walk worthy of the Lord unto all pleasing, being fruitful in every good work and increasing in the knowledge of God, strengthened with all might, according to his glorious power, unto all patience and long-suffering with joyfulness, giving thanks unto the Father, which hath made us meet to be partakers of the inheritance of the saints in light: who hath delivered us from the power of darkness and hath translated us into the kingdom of his dear Son."

In these sublime words of the apostle we have presented to us such a triumph of the spirit over nature as is possible nowhere else but under the power of the Gospel of Jesus Christ. And, what makes this triumph all the grander and more marvelous, is the fact that it is a victory over nature here and now, and that it is not postponed to some far-off and future day. In the collect, also, in short compass, we have the same thought expressed— the misery of our present fallen life, and the glorious hope and the present reality of a new and higher life, whereby we are assured that *"If our earthly house of this tabernacle be dissolved, we have a building of God, a house not made with hands, eternal in the heavens."*

The Church of all ages has at this time commemorated "The Last Things," Death and the Judgment. Through a succession of Sundays the same theme runs, drawing us away from this life to things eternal, and so inviting us to communion with the saints gone before, who are now awaiting us in the kingdom of light. It was out of this feeling of our continued and unbroken fellowship with the blessed saints who are gone before, that a particular festival in the Church Year was set apart as early as the ninth century—the festival of "All Saints." The festival has gone out of use in the Protestant Church, for good reasons, no doubt; and yet we are nevertheless bound to see in it a most profound meaning. The Church is bound to keep up an active sense of "the communion of the saints." The festival of "All Saints" is well calculated to keep alive a sense of such communion; and there can be little doubt that, as a more churchly feeling comes to assert itself, there will be a resuscitation of this festival. We can easily see the importance of such a festival in which the Church below recognizes one communion in Christ for all saints, at least in two important respects:

I. It is adapted to meet the common natural want of the human spirit in regard to those who have died and passed away. The Church Year is not so arranged as to ignore that feeling. The desire to keep up a communion of some kind with departed loved ones is a natural, a universal feeling, found in all times and ages. This feeling Christianity takes up and makes provision for. The social sentiment is one of the grandest distinctions of our human life. We cannot separate ourselves even from those who are dead and gone. And just in this feeling do we find one of the strongest arguments for our immortality. Even in the heathen world is this felt, and of course where the natural life is cultivated, as it is in all Christian and civilized countries, that feeling becomes stronger still, and demands a satisfaction. In this way we are exalted above the animal. We are, by constitution, social. No man is a man, nor can he be said to have the feeling of a man, except as his life is interwoven with the lives of others.

Now, there is no reason why this feeling should not be taken up by Christianity. The few short years of social life we pass here on earth with humanity are not enough. To say that this law of our life, that ever reaches out thus to such sociality, is forever and forever cut off by death is against all reason and philosophy. Hence it is that we rear monuments over the graves of our dead, reminding us of their presence, and giving us the feeling that they are not gone forever, but in some way or other are here present with us still.

There were, in the early Church, festivals in remembrance of the dead, which were in the nature and partook of the character of sacramental services, more or less; and these were undoubtedly the historical ground for the single festival of "All Saints." We said a moment ago that this festival began in the ninth century, but the idea of it was active from the very beginning. There was, in the early Church, a disposition to hold this communion with the saints very prominent, but as these observances were at first scattered through the year, and so found inconvenient, one day was set aside in which the whole Church throughout the world was brought to recognize the union of "All Saints" on earth and in heaven.

II. There is an actual demand for some such kind of public worship. It is demanded for the support of our faith. Faith is not mere thought. No doctrinal knowledge can be sufficient, nor the exercise of any power or faculty of the soul that does not bring before us Christ, as a living presence incarnate, so that we can say, "Thou art the Christ." The whole Christian life depends on that kind of faith. It unites us with Christ. "This is the work of God, that ye believe on him whom he hath sent." No other sentiment will do, for that is the bond of union and direct felt contact with Christ. Now, faith in Him does not preclude faith in His redeeming work. He is not to be regarded as isolated, or as in any wise standing aloof from His people. Some seem to think that it detracts from the dignity of our Lord to believe in the Church, which is "his body," we are told, "the fulness of him that filleth all in all." His life is ever flowing forth into the Church, of which He is the animating power, the ever-living Head. What an organism that would be, in which the head should stand isolated and separate from the members! The head is the head just because it stands in union with the members. Our Lord Jesus Christ is not sundered from the Church at present in the world. We cannot, consequently, at all truly believe in Christ without at the same time believing in His Church, in which His glorified life is ever manifesting itself.

This thought, however, must extend also to the saints in heaven. The Church on earth is but a small part of the Church; and those departed are in the same relation to the Church as before. As we cannot believe in Christ without believing in His Mystical Body here below, neither can we believe in Him without believing also in the communion of saints above. We are to *believe* in it. No mere *thought* will do, here again as before. A faith is necessary. If we do not believe in the Church above, we do not believe in the Church below. We cannot believe in a fragment of the Church any more than in a fragment of a body. This, of course, transcends the natural understanding—all here is a sublime mystery for the apprehension of faith.

The cultivation of sympathy with departed believing spirits is a complement of our faith in Christ. We cannot believe in the Head without believing in the body.

And it is not unreasonable to think that our departed friends are affected by our sympathy here. There is such a feeling in the Christian heart which will not be ignored and cannot be crushed out. However this may be, the cultivation of such a feeling is much for us. It won't do to say that we need no circuitous help from the saints, but that we must go straight to Christ Himself. That sounds well; but when we come to see in the kingdom of grace a *real* economy, then do we come to feel that we do need the sympathy of those gone before us as well as of those still with us in the body here on earth. What should we say of that kind of Christianity which should profess to have no need of sympathy and fellowship with believers here? That should say we have all we need in Christ? Our human life can't be made complete except in a social form, and how should it be completed in Christianity, which is its highest form, independently of all social feeling and social relationship? In proportion as we meditate on our friends gone before, we find ourselves drawn away from the vanity of the things in this world to the abiding reality of things unseen and eternal. "Wherefore, seeing we are compassed about with so great a cloud of witnesses, let us lay aside every weight, and the sin which doth so easily beset us, and let us run with patience the race that is set before us, looking unto Jesus, the author and finisher of our faith."

November 5, 1871.

The Third Sunday before Advent.

THE PERSON OF CHRIST THE CENTRAL OBJECT OF FAITH.

John vi. 28–29.

" *Then said they unto him, What shall we do, that we might work the works of God? Jesus answered and said unto them, This is the work of God, that ye believe on him whom he hath sent.*"

HERE we have the sense of the Gospel in a single proposition, and that from the lips of our Saviour Himself. In order to understand rightly what this proposition means, it is necessary to observe first, the implied and actual contrast here presented between the revelation of God through His Son, and all knowledge of God acquired simply by the natural reason. We are required to believe on Him whom God hath sent, that is, on Jesus Christ, His Son, whose person is the most perfect manifestation of the being of God; but in this requirement there is an implied reference to the revelation of God in the world of nature. That there is such a revelation we see in the Bible—"The heavens declare the glory of God, and the firmament sheweth his handywork." St. Paul says that the heathen were without excuse: "because when they knew God they glorified him not as God, neither were thankful; but became vain in their imaginations, and their foolish heart was darkened." And it is with a quiet reference to this outward manifestation of God's being and presence in the world, that our Saviour exclaims, "This is the work of God, that ye believe on him whom he hath sent." That such a work and such a belief might be rendered possible, it was needed that there should be something further than that revelation which exists in the world of nature. A new manifestation must be made from heaven. God's being and presence must be brought to confront men in a manner different from that with which men had previously been acquainted.

This is the idea of revelation, in the Bible sense of the word. It presents itself in the character of a progressive movement, beginning with the fall and carried forward by the patriarchs and prophets to the final and full revelation in the person of Christ. This movement widens as it advances, and consists not merely in words, but in acts and deeds. God manifested Himself to Noah before the flood, to Moses, Abraham, and to the later prophets; and such a manifestation in every case involved an act on the part of God. It was a stepping out from eternity, so to speak, on God's part into the bosom of our humanity, an inbreathing of Himself into human existence.

All this however, was but a preparation for the one full revelation of Himself when He sent His Son into the world. But this sending of His Son was not like the sending of an angel down from heaven to earth, as the angel Gabriel, for example, was sent to Zacharias to announce the birth of John the Baptist, or to the Virgin Mary to announce the incarnation of the Son of God. In Jesus of Nazareth there was "the brightness of God's glory and the express image of his person." There was in Him the actual living union of the divine and the human natures. The incarnation was thus the highest possible revelation, the culmination of the whole process and movement of all preceding revelation, and of all previous revelations considered as more or less definitely marked stages in the one continuous and unbroken line of revelation, which were foreshadowings of that which was full and final in the person of Christ. On this ground Christ proclaimed Himself "The light of the world," "The way, the truth and the life." It was because of this that He declared, "No man cometh unto the Father but by me." And again, "No man hath seen God at any time. The only begotten Son, which is in the bosom of the Father, he hath declared him." And yet again, "Have I been so long time with you, and yet hast thou not known me, Philip? He that hath seen me hath seen the Father." That shows what was in Christ, and how He transcended immeasurably all that revelation of God which is in the world of nature, and all preceding revelation made by the agency of prophets and holy men of old.

"He that hath seen me, hath seen the Father." All religion, then, culminates in an apprehension of this revelation, in knowing Christ, and in knowing God in Christ. All true Christianity resolves itself into the knowing, not of the doctrines of Christ, nor of passages of the Bible, nor even of the whole of the Bible, but of Christ Himself as the full and final manifestation of God. The knowledge of the Bible and of doctrines comes afterward. If we imagine that by the Bible, or by texts of Scripture, or by picking out the doctrine of justification by faith, and by studying any or all of them, we have Christianity, we only miserably deceive ourselves. We must first be in Christ, who is Alpha and Omega. "This is eternal life, that they might know thee, the only true God, and Jesus Christ whom thou hast sent." Christ here means to join together these two, the knowing of Christ and the knowing of God. But the naturalist says—"that they might know thee, the only true God and "—the constitution of the world! But Christ came from above, not from beneath. He is the great and true missionary from the supernatural home of Jehovah. Hence the Apostle St. John says, " We know that the Son of God is come "—because His presence was a full manifestation of God. " We know "—we do not think, merely—" We know that we are of God, and the whole world lieth in wickedness. And we know that the Son of God is come, and hath given us an understanding that we may know him that is true; and we are in him that is true, even in his Son Jesus Christ. This is the true God, and eternal life." This is plain language. The possession of eternal life depends upon a knowing by faith, and not upon a knowing by thinking. The natural philosopher founds it on God-consciousness, but so far as God comes to be known to him at all, it is by speculation, by ratiocination, by scientific processes. But if revelation be supernatural, we must have a supernatural organ to apprehend it, to know God: which organ is faith. Faith is indispensable for the apprehension of supernatural and eternal things. It is the foundation or ground for knowing God. Hence the Saviour says, " This is the work of God, that ye believe."—The work is not some speculation or theory or doctrine about God, but such a faith in Him as shall lead to such a knowledge of Him as we can acquire in no other manner whatsoever.

Now, under this universal view of the proposition, there are two general thoughts involved, seemingly of an opposite character, but really opposite only in the sense that they are on opposite sides of the same truth—

I. The proposition excludes any work of ours as being good for the purposes of our salvation. The Jews asked,

"What shall we do that we might work the works of God?" meaning thereby the ordinary works of morality. The answer of our Saviour plainly implies that no other work is co-ordinate with that of "believing on him whom he hath sent." Morality there may be without faith, but it cannot minister to salvation. So it is with our natural morality, our common human self-sacrifice, and even zeal for religion. As St. Paul says, a man "may bestow all his goods to feed the poor, and give his body to be burned," and yet if he have not charity, "it profiteth him nothing."

II. On the other hand, however, it is wrong to suppose that this work means nothing more than merely to believe. That would be a wrong view of justification by faith—a making of the means an end. Some talk as if it were a purely magical act on the part of heaven by which they are set in right relation to God. And sometimes men take the ground that being justified by faith there is no need of good works or morality. That is an abstract view of justification by faith, and is a grand heresy. There is no dead justification like that in the whole economy of salvation. Justification is a creative power, a divine thought, which becomes a part of a man's being, a germ of a new order of life. God sends forth His Spirit into our hearts, "whereby we cry, Abba, Father." Faith calls forth love as a response to the benevolence of heaven. Faith renews the soul so that it may exercise patience in the race. Our Saviour's expression, "This is the work of God," takes in all other works. Humility, love, temperance in all things, become Christian graces. But outside or independently of Christianity, these can never become such. In this case they tend only to health and happiness in this world.

In this respect good works are related to faith as are the limbs and fruit of a tree to the germ which produced it.

Out of the many practical lessons which we may here learn, we can notice only two or three.

The first—which is very important—is, that we can now see what is the fundamental power in our Christian experience, without which there can be no title to the name Christian. That power rests in something beyond ourselves, not in anything in ourselves. This is very plain and simple, and yet it is a most important distinction in theology, and in all experimental religion.

Christian experience and personal activity are indeed facts which may not be ignored. There must be repentance. Believing is an effort of the will, and often requires a great struggle. Our Christian life is often compared to a battle, or a race requiring the greatest endurance and exertion. Our Christian life is indeed intensely subjective, and can go forward only in us, and by our hearty co-operation and our vigorous activity. We make all account of experimental piety by which men take the kingdom of heaven by violence.

But it is, nevertheless, a most sad mistake to suppose that Christianity consists in feelings, and in inward states or frames of the mind. It is sometimes thought that by passing through an inward process, by feeling as if suspended over a yawning abyss of perdition and ruin, relief may be found for the troubled soul. This state of mind is always followed by a reaction, by a collapse, and this makes room for an experience or sensation of enlargement; then the imagination comes in—and this is called conversion. Now, we do not mean to say that such experiences are always fallacious and unreliable. What we are concerned to know, in judging of such cases, is this—what is the ground or foundation on which such experiences rest? "Beloved," says St. John, "believe not every spirit, but try the spirits, whether they are of God: because many false prophets are gone out into the world. Hereby know ye the Spirit of God: every spirit that confesseth that Jesus Christ is come in the flesh is of God." This brings us to the consideration of the essential point here, that the primary and moving power in every believer's experience must lie outside of the believer, not as doctrine but as the personal Christ. "Every spirit that confesseth that Christ is come"—and that consists not in a notion, or in an imagination, but in a steady and unwavering faith. There is no faith where people cannot tell what the object of faith is. Without faith, imagination is all. Having no faith, what do people believe in? First, they believe they are sinners. But, as we have seen in the case of faith, it requires a supernatural power to believe that. What then is faith concerned with, in the supposed case? Why, next they believe that if they become converted they will be saved: but that belief again rests only on a natural and not at all upon a supernatural ground. Last of all, having undergone a certain state of feeling, they come to experience a reaction in the nature of a pleasurable state which, with psychological necessity, follows all such feelings, and they then substitute this pleasurable state for faith! But, in all this, where is the *object* on which to rest faith? Faith must have an object; and that object must be supernatural; it must come from above, not from below, from heaven not from earth. That object we find only in that revelation which God has made of Himself in the person of His Son. The only object of Christian faith is Christ. And you must believe on *Him*, not on His works apart from Him, as objects of faith. A man may say, "I believe in the atonement," or again, "I believe in the inspiration of the Scriptures"—yet, if he does not believe first of all in the incarnation, as the full and final manifestation of God in the person of His Son, he cannot truly believe in any doctrine. He must begin at the beginning: his faith must begin with the root, the origin and source of all.

This is simple enough, yet it is often lost sight of, Jesus Christ is Himself the object of all Christian faith. We do not mean to say that faith has but one object, viz: Christ in the incarnation. Faith has to do with all that follows the incarnation, and all that grows forth naturally from it, as set forth in the Creed. Believing in that, you must and will believe also in The Holy Ghost, and the Church, which with all the other supernatural facts in the Creed, are mysteries for faith. As we come to an apprehension of the meaning of an object of faith, so we come to see the difference between faith and a notion or imagination. This act of faith involves an apprehension of Jesus Christ. In this way we learn rightly to esteem the Apostles' Creed, which was the expression of the faith of the Christian Church in the first centuries. And in this way also we can understand the necessity that the various articles of the Creed should occupy the place they do. The Creed cannot be turned around in any way. It must be as it is, all the articles springing forth from the person of Christ, as the radii from the centre of a circle. The Creed is the norm of our faith, and by it, our faith may be tested, and strengthened. There is no other way: we must fall in with the plan of God, as set forth in the Creed, and as sanctioned by the custom of the Church in all ages.

November 7, 1869.

The Second Sunday Before Advent.

THE VOICE OF WISDOM.

Proverbs viii, 1-10.

"Doth not Wisdom cry? And Understanding put forth her voice? She standeth in the top of the high places, by the way in the places of the paths. She crieth at the gates, at the entry of the city, at the coming in at the doors: Unto you, O men, I call, and my voice is to the sons of man."

WISDOM and understanding here, as elsewhere, both in the Old and the New Testament, personify the idea of Religion, which idea is full and perfect only in the person of our Saviour. In every age His presence in the world may be recognized, not only in different modes of revelation, but also in the general sense and meaning of the world. The voice of Wisdom has been heard crying in all ages, and the burden of her cry ever is, "O ye simple, understand wisdom; and ye fools, be ye of an understanding heart."

We shall consider some of the different ways in which Wisdom speaks to men.

In the first place God (or Wisdom) speaks to us through the natural world. There is a deep, inward, living connection between nature and religion. There is an Intelligence shining through the whole natural world, and a right state of mind on our part is all that is wanting to insure a proper apprehension of it. Our Saviour made frequent appeals to nature in His parables and in His teachings generally, not simply as a convenient commentary on the spiritual world, but as a mirror reflecting the images of spiritual things; as something so constitutionally one with the world of mind or spirit, that to His all-seeing vision there was ever and always the expression of something far greater and grander than men ordinarily see in it.

But not only does God, or Christ, or Wisdom, speak to us in nature. The same great Voice is heard also in history, consisting of a moral world grounded in nature. History is possible only in the world of mind, or spirit; a world that is akin to the divine Spirit; and we must admit that God is present in this world of mind or spirit far more than He is present in the world of nature. History reflects a sense of divine things, and gives the most unmistakable tokens of the presence and operations of God. No man can study the constitution of his own mind or ethical life, or the ethical life of a community, without feeling himself confronted by a spirit more powerful than is to be found in the world of nature; and when he enters upon the study of the still broader field of humanity, considered as a whole, what a wide meaning does he not find there.

In the third place, Wisdom is heard to speak in the direct intuitional moral sense which every man carries in his own spirit. The address of Wisdom from this quarter is something quite different from that which we have already considered; for in nature and in history the voice of Wisdom is heard from without, originating in an objective form of existence; but when we turn our thoughts inward upon ourselves, not in the way of logical reflection, but in the way of intuitional perception, then it is pre-eminently that that voice is heard, a voice from the heavenly world, a voice from God. Every man carries this in himself. He may make it a study in the case of others, when it will be found to possess great force; but it is especially and emphatically in his own spirit that he hears the voice of God. " There is a spirit in man, and the inspiration of the Almighty giveth them understanding." There is in every man a consciousness of God which is as original and as fundamental as is the consciousness of self; and this is the most direct and the most cogent argument for the existence of God that may anywhere be found. If that fails, or is ignored, then indeed is the light in the man turned to darkness. But this consciousness of God not only involves an intuitional perception of His omnipresence but what is more, it also leads to a direct and immediate conviction of His spirituality and holiness. To this knowledge we do not come by any process of reflection, but directly in our own consciousness. And this is emphatically the voice of Wisdom, the voice of God in the soul, which can never be silenced. Even amongst the heathen that voice is heard. It makes itself felt and acknowledged wherever there is a human spirit, and this voice, this sounding forth day and night in every soul, is no doubt what is meant by our text, " Doth not Wisdom cry ? and understanding put forth her voice ? "

There is, however, a fourth form in which the voice of God challenges us even in a still more powerful way. The different methods in which we have so far considered Wisdom as speaking to man, would not be intelligible if her voice did not utter itself in yet another form, viz. in the form of a distinct and positive revelation ; such as was that voice which was heard amid the thunders of Mt· Sinai, in the declarations of the prophets, in the record of the Bible, and above all as that voice reaches its highest possible expression in the person of the Son of God, concerning whom the voice of God Himself from heaven declared, "This is my beloved Son in whom I am well pleased. Hear ye him."

Such is the process of revelation, starting away back in the first ages of the world, and perfecting itself in our Saviour. And for us especially, who live in the world since the incarnation, and who stand in the full meridian blaze of the Sun of Righteousness, is this voice full of authority, meaning and power. It is in this form that the voice of Wisdom now cries to men. "God who at sundry times and in divers manners spake in time past unto the fathers by the prophets, hath in these last days spoken unto us by his Son." And this voice in revelation is heard not only when we read the Bible, or when we hear the word of God preached; it has assumed an objective character also in the permanent constitution of the Christian community. Men that never pray, nor read the Bible, nor even attend church, are still compelled to hear the voice of Wisdom crying to them in the life of every Christian man, woman or child they meet. That Voice speaks in every spire pointing heavenward, and in every grave telling of a world beyond.

The following are some of the practical observations that may be made with profit on this subject:

How utterly inexcusable men are in the broad light of Christianity, for neglecting or rejecting this voice! Men often imagine that there is much apology for them because this voice comes from an unseen world, which is so dark, mysterious, and far away; and that because of this there is some excuse for a want of piety on their part, and for such a tenacious clinging to this world, and for shutting out from them all consideration of a world to come. But men are not cut off from the world to come. They are bound to it, as with hooks of steel, and are constantly confronted by it. And although that voice is not a loud voice for the outward sense, yet it is loud and clear for that sense which is within. In this respect, it is a voice of One "standing in the top of the high places, by the way in the places of the paths." It is the Voice of One "crying at the gates, at the entry of the city, at the coming in at the doors: Unto you, O men, I call; and my voice is to the sons of man." So St. Paul says of the heathen, that they were "without excuse, because that when they knew God, they glorified Him not as God, neither were thankful; but became vain in their imaginations; and their foolish heart was darkened." They thought they were following the highest wisdom; they thought they had an excuse. So it is with sinners universally, and in every age (and especially in our own), when they are confronted by this great voice, "If thine eye be single"—(Oh, what a world of meaning there is in this declaration of our Saviour's!)—"thy whole body shall be full of light; but if thine eye be evil," (turbid, distorted, distempered), "thy whole body shall be full of darkness. If therefore the light that is in thee"—("the light that is *in thee*," mark; not, as the infidel says, the light that is *out of* thee, on the outside of thee)—"if the light that is in thee be darkness, how great is that darkness!"

Another reflection is this: if men are without excuse, then they will perish. Their punishment rests on themselves. It might be imagined, and it sometimes is, that men may throw the blame on God. But in the great day of judgment, there will be no room for any extenuation of their crime in the presence of the Hosts of Holiness by whom they will then be surrounded. We have a plain declaration of their utter and awful rejection by the Lord at many places in the Scriptures; and very notable is that statement of it in the first chapter of this book of Proverbs, where Wisdom is represented as "crying without"—not in a secret place, in a closet; but openly and publicly, "in the streets," "in the chief place of concourse," "in the openings of the gates"—and saying, "How long, ye simple ones, will ye love simplicity? And the scorners delight in their scorning, and fools hate knowledge. Turn you at my reproof; behold I will pour out my spirit unto you." But now mark the tremendous and awful threat which follows this gracious invitation—" Because I have called and ye refused; I have stretched out my hand, and no man regarded; but ye have set at nought all my counsel, and would none of my reproof; I also will laugh at your calamity, I will mock when your fear cometh."

November 14, 1869.

The Sunday before Advent.

THE SECOND COMING OF OUR LORD.

The Epistle Lesson for the Day.—2 Peter iii. 3-14.

" Knowing this first, that there shall come in the last days scoffers, walking after their own lusts, and saying, Where is the promise of his coming ? for since the fathers fell asleep, all things continue as they were from the beginning of the creation."

THIS Scripture lesson has been very appropriately chosen for our meditation on the last Sunday in the Church Year. The Church Year closes with a consideration of "the last things"—death, judgment, heaven, hell: whereby we are made to feel the vanity and frailty of all things earthly; which is an impression quite in harmony with the drear and desolate character of the closing part of the natural year; the sombre days of November being well adapted for Christian faith to realize the vanity of this world and the reality of a better and a higher world to come.

Our lesson to-day has reference to the end of the world, but presents this, not as it is regarded by the naturalistic and humanitarian thinking of men, but as the accompaniment or the consequence of the second coming of the Son of Man. It is not possible to exercise faith in His first coming without also going on to believe in His second coming. This is the sense of the Creed, where it is said, "I believe in Jesus Christ, His only begotten Son, our Lord, who was conceived by the Holy Ghost, born of the Virgin Mary, . . . ascended into heaven . . . whence He shall come again to judge the quick and the dead." The two ends of our Saviour's mediatorial work are so intimately joined together in one living, organic process, that His second coming of necessity occupies a very large place in the Gospels, as well as in the Epistles of Paul, Peter and John generally. All this serves to show what a strong hold the fact of the second coming of our Lord had taken upon the faith of the Church in Apostolic times—a faith which stands in striking contrast with the prevailing indifference or positive skepticism on the subject at the present day.

The Epistle Lesson dwells upon the destruction of the present order of things, and points forward and upward to another and a higher order. In the thirteenth verse of the first chapter of this Epistle, the writer says, "Yea, I think it meet, as long as I am in this tabernacle, to stir you up by putting you in remembrance." St. Peter was now an old man, and did not expect in his day to see the coming of Christ, yet he wishes to remind those to whom he is writing of the promises and the certainty of the second advent of our Lord. In the sixteenth verse of the same chapter he says, "For we have not followed cunningly devised fables, when we made known unto you the power and coming of our Lord Jesus Christ, but were eye-witnesses of his majesty." The "coming" here spoken of was not the coming in the flesh, the Incarnation, nor the coming of the Holy Ghost on the day of Pentecost, but the actual coming of Jesus Christ a second time, in His own glorified person, with the holy angels of God; this being the full and final completion of the Gospel, in the only form in which it could be completed. St. Peter says he had been an eye-witness of our Saviour's majesty—but when, and where? On the Mount of Transfiguration when, surrounded by majestic presences from the invisible and eternal world, he was overcome by the unutterable glory of the Saviour, he and the other two disciples being overshadowed by the cloud, from the bosom of which came a voice saying, "This is my beloved Son: hear him." This had so fastened itself upon the mind and memory of the disciple that he could never forget it. He had beheld the glorious epiphany of Christ with his own senses; had seen it with his own eyes, and heard it with his own ears; and in this epiphany the Lord did not pass out of and beyond this world into the heavenly world, but for a time passed into a higher, glorified state of human existence. The mediatorial life of Christ stands in close connection with our fading, failing, dying human life, and is not to be regarded as being separated from it, so as to become a mere abstraction for our thought. He is our Mediator not in any outward or mechanical way, but because He ever stands in living, organic relation to our humanity, which is now glorified in His person. Even while still in the flesh, the three disciples were admitted to behold this glorious epiphany of a new and higher order of life to which human nature had been raised in Him. Only six days before this He had said, "Verily I say unto you that there be some of them that stand here, which shall not taste of death till they have seen the kingdom of God come with power;" the reference being to this glorious manifestation of His majesty and power.

It is upon this general ground that in the closing part of this chapter, St. Peter urges those to whom he is writing, not to give up the hope of His second coming. Concerning this concluding fact in the scheme of redemption there was, even at that early day already, no small amount of infidelity. Men said, scoffing and mocking,

"Where is the promise of his coming? for since the fathers fell asleep, all things continue as they were from the beginning of the creation." There is no sensible evidence or tangible proof of a new and higher order of things breaking in upon the world that now is; things in the present order show no tendency whatever to bring such a result to pass. And so men in that day, as men in this day, rejected altogether the doctrine of a final consummation or catastrophe of the whole present mundane order.

In our time, even more than in St. Peter's time, this same way of thinking and speaking prevails—even in the Church it is not seldom found. Men conceive of our common human life as carrying within it all that is necessary to bring about all that is promised in the Gospel, with the assistance of God's blessing. It is thought, and indeed openly claimed by many, that the world is making a more or less rapid approximation to the coming of the millennium in a purely natural way, by the operation of natural agencies, forces and powers; by the triumphs of mind over matter, by the discoveries of science, by the general diffusion of knowledge and the education of the whole world to a higher plane of intelligence. This is the complacent creed of the naturalist, of the political economist, and is the view held also by a large part of the theology of the present day, the supposition being that nature, assisted by divine grace, will somewhere in the future effloresce into the millennium. It is a very plausible doctrine, a very captivating belief. Men are so easily and so powerfully impressed by the onward course of the merely natural world (including in that term not only outward material nature, but the moral and intellectual life of man, both individually and collectively)—

they are so captivated by the magnificent sweep of human progress from age to age, that they are very easily led to this false conclusion.

The argument of St. Peter here is designed to draw men away from all such false humanitarian conceptions, and to assert a positive breaking in upon the present order of things from above and beyond. This is evidently the purpose of the Apostle in this entire chapter. Some persons in reading this chapter think that the Apostle is here referring to death. But death cannot be identified with the coming of Christ. Death is not something positive, but negative. It is no object of faith, and cannot be; and faith must always have an object on which to rest. How then could the Apostle present that as the object of our faith which presents nothing solid and positive for our faith to rest upon? No. St. Peter here presents to our faith a most sublimely real, objective fact in the scheme of redemption; one that is of such overpowering significance as to sink all nature, and even death itself, into nothing when once compared with it—the glorious appearing of the Son of Man coming in the clouds of heaven, having all the holy angels of God with Him.

Although the Apostle did not expect to see the coming of Christ in his day, he did not allow this to shake his faith. If only the reality of that coming be impressed on men, little matter about the exact time. The day of the Lord will come suddenly, as if it were to come this year, or this day, when men are not all looking for it or expecting it. "Wherefore, beloved, seeing ye look for such things, be diligent that ye may be found of him in peace, without spot and blameless."

November 21st, 1869.

The Sunday before Advent.

THE SECOND COMING OF OUR LORD.

The Epistle Lesson for the Day.—2 Peter iii. 3–14.

(With especial reference to Verses 10–14.)

" *But the day of the Lord will come as a thief in the night; in the which the heavens shall pass away with a great noise, and the elements shall melt with fervent heat, the earth also and the works that are therein shall be burned up.*"

THIS passage of Scripture gathers up unto itself the general sense of the lessons for the day. Both the Gospel and the Epistle lesson for this day look to the second advent, in which the present dispensation of the grace of God shall reach its culmination, corresponding thus to the end of the Church Year. It is worthy of remark, we may observe, that we cannot take up a single epistle of St. Peter or St. John without finding in it a reference to this great and final conclusion of the work of redemption. The parable of the ten virgins, being the Gospel lesson for this day, looks to this, not in a general, vague manner, but specifically as to the coming of the Son of Man. That is the sense also of the Epistle lesson for the day. The whole exhortation of the Apostle in this second chapter is to look for and to await the coming of Christ. The vision of Christ vouchsafed to the holy Apostle, St. Peter, on the Mount of Transfiguration, was evidently in his mind at the time of the writing of this epistle, as we see from the words (i. 16–18): "For we have not followed cunningly devised fables, when we made known to you the power and coming of our Lord Jesus

Christ, but were eye-witnesses of his majesty. For he received from God the Father honor and glory when there came to him such a voice from the excellent glory, This is my beloved Son, in whom I am well pleased." This vision of Christ in His glory was undoubtedly to the Apostle a representation and exhibition of the ultimate triumph of Christ in His coming to judge the world.

The second advent forms an essential part of the Creed. It is not something accidental or adventitious, but something essential to its substance. It would not be complete without it. As soon as we see the relation of the Logos to the first creation, we are shut up to this conclusion of the second coming as the final redemption of the present order of things. The second coming of our Lord is a constituent element or factor of His redeeming work. It is not mentioned simply here and there, and as it were by the way, in the Gospel narrative and in the epistles; but it is so interwoven with the whole scheme of redemption as to make it evident at once that it is essential to the entire conception of it. All the promises and warnings of the New Testament are conditioned, more or less, by the idea of Christ's second coming. All Christians are addressed as "waiting for the coming of our Lord Jesus Christ."

So, also, this second coming of our Lord finds a necessary place in the Creed, which, without it, would indeed be incomplete, for this evidently is the end and consummation of the work of Christ. He shall come to judge. This judgment is not something, as many Christians often think, far off and vague. It is an object of faith, and cannot be disconnected from what precedes it in the order of redemption. If we admit and accept the first article of the Creed, we are bound to go on to the conclusion, and accept this also as the necessary and logical consummation of the whole.

Thus we are prepared measurably to see something of the nature of this great mystery. As a necessary outgrowth of the first advent, we may consider what the second advent is not.

It is not the coming of the Holy Ghost. "I will not leave you orphans. I will come unto you." So said Christ to His sorrowing disciples on the eve of His departure from them. True, that was a coming of Christ; but it was not the second advent.

Then again, the second coming is very different from the death of the individual. Many persons confound the two. Death is the end of our life, through which we pass into another world: and some say that this is the coming of Christ. It is thought that death brings a man into a certain fixed and definite relation to Christ, and it is therefore imagined that our Lord had reference to this when He said, "Watch, for ye know neither the day nor the hour wherein the Son of Man cometh." For the real believer it is thought that this is a coming of Christ to deliver him finally and forever from all evil. That is a plausible view of the matter, but it is nevertheless a most serious error. It obscures the sense and saving force of this article of the second coming. Death is not a victory, but a curse from which the human spirit instinctively shrinks away, although the Christian faith may and does overcome that feeling. Nevertheless, death is a curse, the result of sin. It is the laying of the hand of God on the sinner in judgment. It is easy to see the difference between the two. Death is not only a curse, whereas the second coming is a blessing, but death is something negative, nothing positive, the mere end of our life, a mere negation. Are we, for even a moment, to confound the second coming of our Lord with a mere negation? No; the second coming of Christ is something positive; a positive fullness, such as was His first advent, and includes in itself the whole force and power of the resurrection and the whole redeeming work of His life. Furthermore, death cannot be an article of faith, but the second coming is. An article of faith is a real, positive, supernatural fact of existence, growing out of the incarnation. Now, death does not come as a result of the incarnation. Death comes from sin, from the first Adam, not from the second. There is nothing supernatural about it, and so we don't need any faith in it. We don't need any faith in death any more than we do in birth. It is a *natural* fact which the slightest experience in life shows us. It is a dark mystery, of course, but nevertheless it is included within the scope of the purely natural. The second coming of our Lord, on the contrary, is a mystery in which the supernatural is made to touch the natural. The eye cannot see it; it cannot be made sure to the senses; it must be self-authenticated to faith in distinction from the natural senses; and so, as is the case with all Christian mysteries, it must strike the natural mind as an absurdity. The whole redeeming work of Christ and all its sublime facts, though eminently rational, yet to the natural man are foolishness. "There shall come in the last days scoffers walking after their own lusts and saying, Where is the promise of his coming?" What has become of it? "All things," in the world of nature, "continue as they were from the beginning of the creation." That is forever, in every age, the language of naturalism, the argument of rationalism.

The argument of the Apostle St. Peter shows that the second advent does transcend the merely natural sense, and so is an object for faith, holding in the mystery of the supernatural world. And his argument is that since the first creation is not demonstrable to the senses, why should the second coming of Christ be, creating the new heavens and the new earth wherein dwelleth righteousness?

In these ways we can easily see how different the second coming is from death. We can never do justice at all to the thought of Christ's second glorious advent by making it identical with our death. It is a profound mystery, reaching down into the depths of the world's life.

We may now see the use of this article of the Creed. It is of practical consequence, as being an object for our faith. Our apprehension of it must be a faith—not a barren speculation about it, or a notion concerning it—but a positive, real faith in it. It was undoubtedly with reference to the difficulty of realizing it in this way that our Saviour was moved to exclaim, "When the Son of man cometh, shall he find faith on earth?" that is, shall He find *this* kind of faith, of which we are speaking, waiting for Him? This is the keystone in the arch of the Christian faith. As there is no complete redemptive work without the second coming, so there can be no perfect faith that does not lay hold on the second coming. What a great thing it is to feel that we are thus confronted and challenged by the high economy of grace in its entire constitution, and to have faith in it! It is, indeed, a great and grand thing to lay hold of these facts by a power utterly transcending thought, so that we may exclaim with Thomas, "My Lord, and my God!"

That is always true of every fact in our Lord's redeeming work, but it seems especially hard to lay hold of this article of the second coming in this way.

We need, however, strongly to lay hold on and to meditate upon this sublime and glorious advent, so that we may stand strong against all gnostic and humanitarian views.

There is a tendency to regard our life as rising upward in a humanitarian way, by virtue of its own power, into a higher life. This is the tendency of all natural science, which seeks to enable man to master all the secrets of nature, and which, beginning in the depths, would scale the heavens. We must beware of that! We feel instinctively that our birth is from the skies, and that thitherward are we bound. It is only when we feel the nothingness of our life that we become sensible of our need of redemption. Yet, this redemption coming through Christ cannot be apprehended by the understanding, but must authenticate itself to faith, and brings with it an evidence higher and stronger than any evidence of science. That sublime thought runs all through this Epistle of St. Peter. He has not "followed cunningly-devised fables;" he has also "a more sure word of prophecy, whereunto ye do well that ye take heed as unto a light that shineth in a dark place, until the day dawn and the day star arise in your hearts."

Then, furthermore, we have in this Epistle Lesson for the day a setting forth of the design of this article of the second coming for the practical purposes of our Christian life. The second coming does not address the fears of believers. It is the winding up of this our present miserable life, and so should not be contemplated with feelings of fear. When that great truth once truly enters into the mind, and takes full possession of the soul, we rise to the power of making nothing of this world, whether as natural, moral or political. Most men, indeed, sooner or later, come to admit that, in a general, poetical and sentimental way, but they do not truly feel it. When once we have anything like a proper apprehension of the sublime fact of the second coming of the Son of Man, the world for us becomes shorn of its power—we are enabled to despise it, to cast it from us, and so to "run with diligence the race that is set before us." This was undoubtedly the feeling of the first early Christians, who thought the world about to come to an end. Therefore were they willing "to suffer the loss of all things" to be made "a spectacle unto the world, unto angels and unto men," and to crown all their other sufferings with martyrdom. The Epistles, taken as a whole, go upon that feeling—"The Lord is at hand, be careful for nothing." And all Christians, in every age, ought to share that feeling, whether in prosperity or adversity. "Our life is hid with Christ in God, and when Christ who is our life shall appear, then shall we also appear" in the glory of a new and higher life. Thus our life is now hid, as it were, for a short time, "and when he shall appear," it shall come forth in the full glory of a new life, "in the new heavens and earth wherein dwelleth righteousness."

November 26, 1871.

A Baccalaureate Sermon.*

NATURE AND GRACE.

John iii. 13.

"No man hath ascended up to heaven, but he that came down from heaven, even the Son of man which is in heaven."

To reach the full sense of this remarkable declaration on the part of our Lord Jesus Christ, we need to have clearly before us the occasion on which it was uttered.

There was a man of the Pharisees, we are told, by name Nicodemus, a member of the Jewish Sanhedrim, and a leading master or teacher in Israel. The same came to Jesus by night, and said unto Him: "Rabbi, we know that thou art a teacher come from God; for no man can do these miracles that thou doest except God be with him."

The object of the address was to draw the Saviour into an exposition of His views and aims, in the prophetical character in which He appeared; and it was prompted by the serious thought, no doubt, that the new prophet might be indeed the Messiah promised to the fathers, and that the time had come possibly for the solemn inauguration of His kingdom. In this feeling Nicodemus was not alone, at that time, among the rulers of his nation. He spake for others as well as for himself: "*We* know, that thou art a teacher come from God!" The miracles performed by Jesus were the seal of His divine mission;

---

* A Baccalaureate Sermon preached to the late Graduating Class of Franklin and Marshall College, on the evening of the last Sunday in June, 1872, in the First Reformed Church of Lancaster, Pa.

and those who sat in Moses' seat, the guardians of the ancient Jewish faith—some of them at least—were inclined to come to an understanding with Him in regard to the kingdom of God He had in His mind, and if it were found satisfactory to join also the weight of their character and influence with Him in bringing it to pass.

All this, however, rested as we can easily see on a radically defective apprehension, both of the person of Christ and of the work for which He had come into the world. The stand-point of Nicodemus, over against the revelation of God in Christ, was that of rationalistic supernaturalism. Christ was for him at most a teacher sent from God, a prophet like unto Moses, holding in His hand an outward commission from heaven, duly certified by His miracles as outward seals. He was a man clothed with divine powers for the accomplishment of a divine work; but the divinity which was perceived to be in Him and with Him, came to no real union with His humanity. This was the defect of the Jewish idea of the Messiah in general; a defect for which there was no effectual help indeed, until Christ Himself appeared as the full object of the Christian faith. Before that the Messianic conception was necessarily dualistic, and the dualism had no power to save itself from ultimate humanitarianism as expressed in the creed of Nicodemus, "Thou art a *man* come from God." It is in substance the Ebionitic heresy, which figures so largely afterwards in the early history of the Christian Church. In the view of such thinking, Christianity could be only a continuation of Judaism out of its own last result and end, and nothing more. The days of the Messiah were to be in some way the efflorescence simply of the Old Testament theocracy, in the midst of outward signs and wonders, into the highest perfection of its own order of life. So Nicodemus, with others of like mind with himself, looked for the advent of the kingdom of God, and mused in his spirit at this time on the possibility that Jesus of Nazareth might be that prophet raised up of God to bring about the restoration of Israel by its means.

To this general wrong posture of mind on the part of the venerable Jewish rabbi, rather than to his somewhat diplomatic speech directly, our Saviour addressed His profoundly soul-awakening reply: "Verily, verily, I say unto thee, Except a man be born again, he cannot see the kingdom of God."

It is unfortunate, certainly, that the Greek term ἄνωθεν in this passage, should be rendered in our version by the adverb *again*, when it signifies in truth, properly and immediately, *from above*. Any birth indeed that is new, however it may be brought to pass, is of course a regeneration, or being born again, and may be properly so named. But plainly it is not just the thought of being born *again*, in the ordinary religious sense of the term regeneration (familiar as this was to the Jewish mind in connection with the Jewish proselyte baptism), that our Saviour here means to press on the attention of Nicodemus; it is rather, instead of this, the thought that lies immediately in the primary sense of the word ἄνωθεν itself, as denoting a birth "from above," from beyond the natural order of the world's life; and His declaration should read accordingly: "Except a man be born from above, he cannot see the kingdom of God." This kingdom was not to be considered a mere last product of the constitution of Judaism in any form; it was the revelation of a new, higher order of life in the world, descending directly from God Himself; and the first condition therefore even of seeing it, or of understanding in any way its true nature, could be nothing less than a principle of new heavenly life proceeding also from God, or in other words a new birth derived from the womb of the kingdom itself which was to be thus known and entered.

That this was our Saviour's meaning is rendered plain from what He adds immediately after: "Verily, verily, I say unto thee, Except a man be born of water and of the Spirit, he cannot enter into the kingdom of God." Here being "born from above" is made equivalent to being "born of the Spirit;" while the conjunction of the water with the Spirit serves of itself to sunder the sense of all previous Jewish purifications and lustrations (ending in the baptism of John), from the higher consecration thus brought into view. The terrestrial symbol was to become full and complete now through actual union with its true celestial sense; according to that word spoken to the Baptist: "Upon whom thou shalt see the Spirit descending, and remaining on him, the same is he which baptizeth with the Holy Ghost." The birth from above is more than the washing of a simply moral or theocratic regeneration even in its highest form; it goes beyond all this; it is a birth not of water only, but "of water and of the Spirit." It is the introduction of a new divine principle into the being of the soul. It is not in any way of nature, or from the powers of man's life existing before itself. As related to all this it is transcendental and supernatural. It is in such view the opposite of all earthly natural birth, a birth literally and strictly *from above*.

The contrast could not be put in stronger terms than it is by what our Lord adds in explanation of it: "That which is born of the flesh is flesh; and that which is born of the Spirit is spirit." The life of nature can have no power to transcend or rise beyond itself. Its birth is the measure of its capabilities whether physical or moral. If man is to attain then to a true divine life, it must be by the coming down of this life into him as something more than flesh. He must be born of the Spirit. Only what is from the Spirit in this way can be itself spirit, capable of having place and part in the kingdom of God.

The necessity of a communion between earth and heaven, between man and God, that should be something more than a moral or spiritual rising simply of the human to the divine in the order of the human itself; the necessity of a real coming down of the divine into the sphere of the human, to make room for such supernatural communion, as the only true idea of the kingdom of God; that is the great thought which governs and underlies throughout the discourse of our Saviour with Nicodemus, and which leads also in the end to the true view of what Christ Himself was as the solution of this problem and the founder of this kingdom. He was no mere teacher come from God, the reporter of divine oracles attested in an outside way by divine miracles. He was nothing less than the very presence of God Himself among men in human form. "We speak that we do know," He says, "and testify that we have seen." He was empowered to tell of heavenly things, not of knowing them in an earthly way by outward testimony or argument, but as one who was Himself an inmate of heaven, and an eye-witness of the things that are there. This was the capacity in which He appeared among men. That was the nature of His mission and work in the world. That was the key to the true and full sense of the Messianic kingdom which He had come to establish, and of which Nicodemus was now present to inquire. So much, and no less, the idea of that kingdom demanded, if it was to be what the need of the world required, a real restoration of man to the lost life of heaven. No such restoration could start from below, from the fallen life of man himself; it must descend upon man from God. "No man," as our text has it, "hath ascended up to heaven, but he that came down from heaven, even the Son of Man which is in heaven."

There is brought into view here what may be termed a fundamental and universal law of our human spiritual life. This is determined in its very nature toward God by a force which can become effectual for its end at the same time only through power descending into it from God. "Thou awakest us to delight in Thy praise," says St. Augustine; "for Thou madest us for Thyself, and our heart is restless, until it rest in Thee."

In a still wider view, indeed, the whole world is in this way carried toward God, as its ultimate end; and its upward movement everywhere is upheld and sustained, in each stage of its rising course, by the energy of a higher existence flowing down into it from above. In other words, final causes everywhere are the actuating soul of efficient causes.

Thus it is that the unorganized elements of nature, air, water, light, heat, force, have their full meaning only in the metamorphosis or transmutation they are made to undergo through the law of life, and first of all the plastic principle of plant life, bringing them into a new and higher mode of existence. And just so it is again that this first and lowest order of organization, the plant world, reaches forth of itself toward that which is above it, the sphere of animal life; into which it has power actually to pass, however, only as it is itself caught up again, by a force descending into it from that superior sphere itself; a force which imparts a new quality, by assimilation, to all the elements that come under its action, and which serves to advance them thus one degree nearer than before to the last grand object of their creation.

But it is the transition of nature from the animal to man, in whom nature transcends itself by rising into the life of mind or spirit, that the law in question comes finally to its clearest manifestation. Here is a metamorphosis or glorification, a sublimation of the world, which surpasses immeasurably all going before, while it throws a sea of light, at the same time, back on the whole movement of creation, revealing what had been in truth the inmost working sense of it from the beginning. But that sense or end (the teleology of the entire cosmos) is now most of all seen to be a power, working down into nature, and lifting it up into its own higher sphere. "There is a *spirit* in man," we are told, "and the inspiration or inbreathing of the Almighty giveth him understanding." It is as joined with this higher principle in man, as transmuted in this way into the spirituality of thought, and made to mirror itself in the human intelligence, that the world in its natural order is, as it were, carried above and beyond itself, and is thus raised to its highest glory in the scheme of creation.

And all this, we now say, is but an analogy and adumbration in the world of nature of the great spiritual law, presented to us by our present subject; the law, whereby the rational nature of man again, in which the lower world becomes complete, is inwardly necessitated to seek its perfection and supreme good also beyond itself and in God; while it is able to do so effectually, at the same time, only as the light and life of heaven are made first to flow down into it for that purpose.

It is not simply the existence of *sin*, as sometimes seems to be imagined, that requires this order. Apart from the fact of the fall altogether, and before the fall, we meet with it in the Garden of Eden. The image of God which belonged to our unfallen nature there, formed of itself for this nature the necessity of its communion with God; while that communion, however, had place only by the coming down of the Divine presence to make it possible. God revealed Himself to our first parents in Paradise, and they heard His voice, we are told, as of one walking and conversing with them in the most immediately personal way.

But if the union of man with God needed even before the fall this bowing of the heavens, this coming down of the divine into the sphere of the earthly and human, to make it a reality and not a mere aspiration or dream, how much more must the same condition be regarded as holding necessarily of what the state of man became after the fall, through which the light that was in him has been turned into darkness, and the strength of his original righteousness, is changed into the melancholy weakness of original sin!

How incompetent he is in such fallen condition to solve the great problem of religion, and thus satisfy the inmost and deepest need of his own being, by rising above himself and entering into true life-communion with the heavenly and divine, is shown abundantly by the history of his efforts and endeavors in this direction from the beginning.

The old mythological story of the earth-born giants

striving to scale the heavens in an outward physical way, by piling high mountains one upon another, is but an image or parable of these struggles, by which humanity thrown upon its own resources has vainly sought in the use of its best powers, through all ages, to rise with inward moral elevation to the true knowledge and possession of the Divine.

Neither in the way of intelligence nor in the way of will, neither in thought nor in life, was the ancient *Paganism* able in any sort to actualize what was felt to be here the inmost sense of religion, and the chief end of man. Its heroes rose to the dignity of demi-gods by their imaginary virtue; its philosophers soared high above the earth by their imaginary wisdom. But in neither case was there any true ascending into heaven, any true bringing down of God and heavenly things into felt union and communion with the life of man on the earth. That was something which no moral Hercules, and no speculative Pythagoras or Plato, had power, even in the least degree, to compass or bring to pass. Virtue in such form, and wisdom in such form, were after all humanitarian only; flesh, born of the flesh, and not spirit, born of the Spirit; which as such accordingly could neither see nor enter into the kingdom of God.

The history of the Pagan world before Christ was in this way a preparation for His advent. It was a grand demonstration of the total inability of the world to fulfil the idea of religion by raising itself to a true knowledge of God; and an argument thus for the necessity of a descending movement on the part of God Himself, a Divine self-revelation on the side of God in the fullest sense of the term, to make such religion possible. It was an experiment indeed, according to St. Paul, for this very purpose. "After that in the wisdom of God," he tells us, 1 Cor. i. 21, "the world by wisdom knew not God, it pleased God by the foolishness of preaching to save them that believe." Christianity came as the easy and simple answer for faith to the question of ages, which for the wisdom of the old Oriental world, the wisdom of Egypt, and the later wisdom of Greece, had been thought long centuries before, a source only of interminable confusion and despair.

But granting all this in the case of the Gentile world before Christ, how does it affect, it may be asked, the case of the *Jewish* world before Christ? Was not the want of the Gentile world actually met there in the form of divine revelation, ages in advance of His advent in the flesh; and was not this a real solution of the great problem of humanity, the uniting of man with God in the way of religion, back altogether of what our Saviour here, in His conversation with Nicodemus, declares to be the only true solution of it, namely: His own personal descent as the Son of Man from heaven?

To this there can be but one answer, if Christ Himself is true. All revelation before Christ was relative and partial only, having its ultimate reality in Him alone; and so all religion in the Jewish form was also only relative and partial, a prolepsis simply as far as it went of the full new birth of Christianity, the "shadow and not the very image" of what it prefigured, that as such could reach its own full completion only beyond this life, and after Christ actually came (Heb. xi. 13, 39, 40). Christ was in the world, as the eternal Logos, before He became incarnate, and so also was the Holy Ghost; but neither one nor the other in the same sense or with like power, as afterwards. The difference was that between Christ coming (or about to come) and Christ actually come; that between the promise of the Holy Ghost, as the power of the new creation in Christ Jesus, and the actual gift or sending of the Holy Ghost, which took place when Christ was glorified, and which could not, we are told, take place before (John vii. 39).

Judaism thus, as we know, was also but a preparation for Christ; not a mere negative preparation indeed like Gentilism; on the contrary a Divinely ordered positive preparation, the very portico of entrance itself, we may say, into the the glorious sanctuary of His presence; but still a preparation only for the Christian fact, and not the full power of the fact itself in its own proper form. What the Baptist says of himself, holds good of the whole dispensation ending in his person. It was the voice of one crying in the wilderness, "Prepare ye the way of the Lord and make His paths straight." It was not the kingdom of God or of heaven, of which our Saviour speaks in His discourse with Nicodemus.

In a profound sense, therefore, the declaration, "No man hath ascended up to heaven, but he that came down from heaven," applies in all its force to the Old Testament prophets no less than to the heroes, lawgivers and sages of the ancient heathen world. Moses, Elias, and Isaiah had been as little able in their time to ascend up to heaven, in the sense of this declaration, as either Zoroaster or Confucius, Pythagoras or Plato. Not even the inspiration of the Holy Ghost, by which they were moved, carried them to any such height as this. They spake as they were thus moved, but the oracles they uttered had not their origin in themselves, and were not drawn directly and immediately from their own knowledge. They could not say of the things of heaven, as Christ does, "We speak that we do know, and testify that we have seen." They performed miracles and uttered prophecies; but no one of them could have dared to say with Jesus Christ: "I am in the Father, and the Father is in me: the words that I speak unto you, I speak not of myself; but the Father that dwelleth in me, he doeth the works."

No one of them could have dared to say, with Him: "I came forth from the Father, and am come into the world; again I leave the world, and go to the Father." Or that other word of like sounding import: "All things are delivered unto me of my Father; and no man knoweth who the Son is, but the Father; and who the Father is, but the Son, and he to whom the Son will reveal him." Speech of this sort, we all feel, would have been horrid blasphemy from any lips other than those of Jesus Christ; whereas proceeding from Him it is felt as only in harmony with His universal character and presence, and produces no shock. He stands alone among the Old Testament prophets; the end of their glorious succession, and yet immeasurably more than all of them put together, as we are expressly told by the last and greatest among them, John the Baptist. "Of his fulness," he says, "have all we received, and grace for grace. For the law was given by Moses, but grace and truth came by Jesus Christ. No man hath seen God at any time: the only begotten Son, which is in the bosom of the Father, he hath declared him."

We have the same broad contrast of relative and absolute revelation brought into view again in the beginning of the Epistle to the Hebrews, where it is said: "God, who at sundry times and in divers manners spake 'in time past unto the fathers by the prophets, hath in these last days spoken unto us by his Son, whom he hath appointed heir of all things, by whom also he made the worlds; who being the brightness of his glory, and the express image of his person, and upholding all things by the word of his power, when he had by himself purged our sins, sat down on the right hand of the Majesty on high."—Heb. i. 1, 2, 3.

This transcendent order of the Saviour's ministry is plainly set forth in what took place at His baptism; when, as He came up out of the water, the heavens were opened unto Him, we are told, the Spirit of God descended upon Him in bodily form, and from above was heard the voice of the Father Himself, saying: "This is my beloved Son, in whom I am well pleased." This it was indeed that proclaimed to John the Baptist the full sense of His Messiahship over against all the inspirations and theophanies of the Old Testament, and enabled that great witness to say: "I saw, and bare record that this is the Son of God." Heaven and earth were joined together in His person. He was the true tabernacle of God among men.

Of like import with this demonstration on the banks of the Jordan was the vision afterwards of Tabor; that high mountain apart into which Jesus brought Peter, James, and John his brother; and where He was transfigured before them, so that His face did shine as the sun, and his raiment was white as the light. In the midst of this splendor, there appeared unto them, it is said, two men, also in shining apparel, which were Moses and Elias; who talked with Him, and spake of His decease which He should accomplish at Jerusalem. And, behold, a bright cloud overshadowed them, the symbol of Jehovah's presence, and behold a voice out of the cloud, which said: "This is my beloved Son, in whom I am well pleased; hear ye him." Here, the secondary and dependent character of the universal Old Testament revelation, as related to Christ, is brought into view in the most solemn and impressive manner. Its great representatives, Moses and Elias, the founder and the restorer of the Law, had ages before ascended to heaven—the last even in an outward chariot of fire, and without the usual form of death. Yet here they appear as owing all their glory to Him who had come after them, and their presence is but the occasion for showing forth the absolutely incomparable majesty which belonged to Him, as the Son of Man, who was at the same time the only begotten Son of God.

These two titles, meeting in the conception of the Messiah, condition each other and come in the end to the same sense.

The law of centralization runs through the whole human life, and finds its end at last only in the idea of a grand central Man, who as such must be at once one and universal, the second Adam, the head and representative of the race in its true ideal perfection. That, and nothing less, is the meaning of the Messianic title *Son of Man*.

But such an ultimate centre of humanity, having power to recapitulate and hold together its universal life as one, must be at the same time more than human, must be the power of a higher divine life revealing itself in and through the human, for the purpose of raising it into real union and fellowship with God. This is what St. Paul has in his mind where he speaks (Eph. i. 10) of the gathering together in one of all things in Christ, both which are in heaven and which are on earth. No simple ascension of the human out of its own sphere, not even the translation of an Enoch or the fiery sublimation of an Elias, could open the way for any such intercourse and communion between earth and heaven. The power making this possible must first of all start from above. The life of God must reach down into the life of man, so as to lift this up into his own higher sphere. So much, and nothing less, is what is signified to us by the Messianic title *Son of God*.

Only the Son of God thus *could* be the Son of Man; and Jesus is the Messiah, because He was in the days of His flesh, and still is, and will always continue to be, the union of these two distinctions, "conceived by the Holy Ghost and born of the Virgin Mary," both God and man in two distinct natures and one person forever.

The central exclusiveness, and absolute completeness, of the mediation of Jesus Christ, are expressed alike in both titles; and faith in the one is necessarily at the same time faith also in the other.

"Rabbi, thou art the Son of God, thou art the king of Israel," exclaimed Nathanael, struck with the first evidence he had of the superior nature of Jesus of Nazareth. Jesus, in reply, intones the correlative significance of what He was on His earthly human side. "Thou shalt see greater things than these," He tells him. "Verily, verily, I say unto you, Hereafter ye shall see heaven open, and the angels of God ascending and descending upon the *Son of Man*." Heaven in free communication with earth; angels ascending and descending between the two otherwise sundered worlds; but all centering in the glorious mystery of the Incarnation, where the Son of God and the Son of Man meet together as one. The descending movement in this way first; only so, however, as to become at once an ascending movement also, raising the life of humanity into real union with the life of God.

"Whom do men say that I the Son of man am?" To this question of our Lord, we are told (Matthew xvi. 14), the common answer ran, "John the Baptist, Elias, Jeremias, or one of the prophets;" humanitarian conceptions all, at best, of the Messiahship required for the full ideal completion of the human race. But for Peter and his fellow-apostles, the Son of Man was infinitely more than this. "Thou art the Christ," they say, "the Son of the living God;" and the answer, as we know, was the heaven-inspired response of faith to the challenge of the divinity itself, which shone forth immediately from His person. They saw and felt in Him, a man who was greater than all men besides. A man, who stood solitary and alone among the children of men, and yet comprehended in Himself the inmost and deepest sense of humanity. A man, in one word, the absolute completeness of whose humanity showed Him to be more than man, revealed in Him and through Him the glory of the higher world, and thus proved him to be the world's true Christ or Messiah, the Son of Man who was at the same time, as such, the only begotten Son of God.

Such in a general view is the order of the Christian salvation, the economy of the kingdom of God, on which our Saviour seeks to fasten the wondering attention of Nicodemus, in the passage we have before us as a text at this time: "No man hath ascended up to heaven, but he that came down from heaven, even the Son of man which is in heaven."

In full symphony with this, we seem to hear St. Paul's

triumphal pæan (Eph. iv. 9, 10) chanted so grandly to the Ephesians: "Now that he ascended, what is it but that he also descended first into the lower parts of the earth? He that descended is the same also that ascended up far above all heavens, that he might fill all things."

Redemption for man, deliverance from the power of sin and death; not in the mode of any outward, superficial change merely wrought from below, through the natural resources of humanity itself, or by the illapse even of heavenly influences coming in to adjust these resources in their own order; but only in the mode of a new divine life, proceeding forth from God in personal form, and taking hold of the fallen life of the world in a real historical way, so as to rescue it from the captivity of Satan and raise it to the light of immortality and heaven: this is what Christianity means, and it is not possible that it can be rightly understood or made of proper practical account in any other view.

From the whole subject allow me now in conclusion, my dear pupils, members of the Graduating Class of 1872, to draw in brief terms a few general lessons of high practical moment, which I ask you to take with you from the solemnity of the present hour as my paternal farewell charge, for the use of your lives in time to come. The lessons you will at once perceive, are not new; they have formed in one way or another the burden of what you have been taught in the way of religion through your whole college course. But they are lessons at the same time which can never grow old, and which it is especially proper therefore to emphasize and enforce upon your attention on this occasion.

1. Christianity is not primarily a doctrine for the

understanding, nor a rule of conduct for the will, but a principle of life for the soul deeper than either understanding or will, and carrying in it the power of a divine regeneration for all that the soul is, or is capable of becoming, in any other view.

2. As *life* in this sense, accordingly, religion is infinitely more than the conception of any supposed natural morality and virtue, which under the name of life is made too often to stand in the room of all religious theory and faith; as when it is said:

> " For points of faith let graceless zealots fight,
> *His* can't be wrong whose life is in the right."

Practice in *that* view is just as little true life, in the deep Christian sense of the term, as knowledge or doctrine. Life in the Christian sense of the term involves faith; for it is a birth from above, which as such cannot be without some apprehension of its own supernal origin and source.

3. So much is comprehended at once in the idea of this supernal birth itself, as it is presented to us in the Gospel. For it is no re-ordering merely of the natural powers of the soul; nor yet any general influence simply of the Divine Spirit upon the human spirit, that the new birth here signifies, as we have now seen from our Saviour's discourse with Nicodemus. On the contrary, what it signifies is incorporation by the power of the Holy Ghost, figured in holy baptism, into the new life which had been brought into the world by the Incarnation of our Lord Jesus Christ; "who, being God of God, very God of very God, dwelling in the bosom of the Father from all eternity, at last when the fulness of the time was come, came down from heaven, and became man, for us

men and for our salvation;" who "was delivered for our offences, and was raised again for our justification;" who, "by his appearing hath abolished death and brought life and immortality to light through the Gospel;" and who, by the sending of the Holy Ghost, and the institution of the Church, has made room for the real, historical and objective presence of this new order of life among His people to the end of time.

4. We cannot then make too much of the Person of Christ, regarded as the principle and ground of the Christian salvation. He is not the mere functionary simply through whom this salvation is administered and made known; He is the very substance and power of the salvation itself; it holds throughout in the constitution of His mediatorial life, which by its very nature has been, and is still, in the most real historical way, the entire mystery of godliness, ordained before all ages for the redemption and glorification of the world. To the question: "What think ye of Christ? whose son is he?" it is not enough for us to respond: "He is the son of David." He must be for us in full earnest at the same time also the Son of the Living God. In other words, He must be to us in His own personal being more than all His heavenly teaching and divine working. These are great, and greatly to be magnified, as the objective matter of Christian faith; but deeper than all this, and before all this, He is Himself the ultimate fundamental object of that faith, and it is only as the entire matter of it is apprehended as growing forth from that in this central view, that any part or portion of it can ever be rightly apprehended under any other view.

5. We are bound thus to allow full scope to the Messianic title *Son of God*, in our conception of Christ and

His work. We may not narrow it into the notion of a mere official dignity; we may not resolve it into the character of a pale Gnostic abstraction. It must be allowed to condition for us practically the height and depth, the length and breadth of the Christian redemption. This redemption can be no accident or after-thought in the economy of creation. It is no figure of speech simply, to parallelize the new creation, as St. Paul does, with the old. It is only our miserably low way of thinking of Christ, that can ever tempt us to any such thought. The principle of the two creations is the same, and the end therefore, here as elsewhere, must have in it not only all, but more than all, the cosmical significance of the beginning. Only the "first-born of every creature" (Col. i. 15, 18) could become also the "first-born from the dead;" the Father being pleased thus "that in him *all* fulness should dwell." The predestination of grace in this way antedates the predestination of nature, having had place in Christ, we are told (Eph. i. 4), "before the foundation of the world." Grace in such view is older than nature, deeper than nature, more comprehensive than nature. Christ is the Alpha and Omega of both, and of both joined together as one. He descended, as the Redeemer of the world, *into the lowest parts of the earth*, that He might ascend up to His work far above all heavens, and so fill all things. The powers of the kingdom of heaven in His hand take hold on the deep places of the earth, the lowest foundations of the world's being and life. They are cosmogonic, world-historical, and world-teleologic in the profoundest and inmost sense of these terms, ending at last in the "new heavens and the new earth wherein dwelleth righteousness."

6. All this, we say, belongs to Christ as the Son of

God; but in all this we are bound again to see and own in Him at the same time, in its full unbroken force, the Messianic dignity of the *Son of Man*. Only as thus gathering up into Himself the absolute and last sense of humanity, could He be at once the deepest and highest sense of the world, the Alpha and Omega of the world's life. He took upon Him the nature of man; had a real human birth; grew in wisdom and virtue as He grew in years; was tempted and tried as we are, only without sin; as a man, wrestled with the curse of sin that lay upon our general race, with death and with him that had the power of death; as a man, triumphed on the cross, went down into hades, rose again on the third day, and finally ascended up on high, leading captivity captive; where He sitteth at the right hand of the Father, and from whence He shall come again, as a man, to judge the quick and the dead (Matt. xxvi. 64; Acts xvii. 31; Rev. i. 7). Through all these stages, and under all these aspects, His humanity challenges our full unfaltering acknowledgment and faith; and the whole power to communicate with it as an earnest reality in this way.

7. True man, without sin, and yet at the same time true God, as our Catechism puts it; or as it runs in the old Athanasian Creed: "God, of the substance of the Father, begotten before the worlds, and man of the substance of His mother, born in the world; perfect God, and perfect man, of a reasonable soul and human flesh subsisting." That is the great mystery of godliness, the mystery of the incarnation of our Lord Jesus Christ, "which, except a man believe truly and firmly," we are told, "he cannot be saved."

8. Such *believing* is determined directly and immediately by the authority of its object, before all power of

understanding the nature and constitution of the mystery itself which is thus embraced. The apprehension of faith is not from knowledge, but in order to knowledge. The fact of the Trinity manifested through the fact of the Incarnate Son of God, goes before the dogma of the Trinity comprehended theoretically in the dogma of the Incarnation; and the faith of the Church was sure of both facts in the beginning, as we know, long before the sense of either was brought to any clear dogmatic expression. And thus it is that universally true Christian faith regards primarily Christ Himself, and not any doctrine of Christ; although Christ is at once for it again the root of all right doctrine, as well as the principle of all right life. To believe in Christ as very God and very man, it is not necessary that I should be able in the first place to see *how* the Divine can be thus inwardly and organically joined with the human in His person. I may feel the full force of the fact as it confronts me in the evangelical history, without being able to understand it. Theological science has not yet been able to express it in full; perhaps will never be able to do so in this world. It is a study even for angels; and how then should it be otherwise than largely incomprehensible for men? But faith here waits in no sense for theological science. It finds the whole Gospel in the personal Christ Himself, and finds it to be here at the same time the wisdom of God and the power of God unto salvation.

9. The saving power of faith lies thus in what it embraces, which is ultimately always "Christ come in the flesh," and not in any worth of faith itself otherwise considered. Its whole worth holds in its office of apprehending in a real way the objective revelation which

God has been pleased to make of Himself in His Son Jesus Christ; which revelation, thus apprehended, Christ Himself assures us (John xvii. 3), is nothing less than life eternal. The Christian salvation in this way, while it ends in subjective experience, draws all its force primarily from realities which are beyond and high above this experience. There can be no true experimental piety in the Christian sense, that is not the product of these heavenly and supernatural realities, working upon the soul and taking hold upon the life from their own objective sphere. The objectivities of the Gospel, as we may call them, are in this way of more account than its subjectivities. They are emphatically those "powers of the world to come," that are spoken of in the Epistle to the Hebrews as entering into all Christian experience; powers, which flow down into men from above, issuing from Christ, the Lord of life and glory, and mediated for the apprehension of faith by the power of the Holy Ghost through the word and sacraments. Forth out from the prison-house of self, and away from the transitory, perishing show of things seen and temporal, through the aspect or look of faith continually turned toward Jesus, the great forerunner and champion of the Christian faith; that is the wisdom of the saints, the virtue of the just, and the only law of deliverance from this present evil world. "For this is the victory that overcometh the world," according to Saint John, "even our faith. Who is he that overcometh the world, but he that believeth that Jesus is the Son of God?" (1 John v. 4, 5).

10. Let us consider well, then, that we may always firmly hold fast, what is the true order of nature and grace, the right relation of earth to heaven, or of things

which are seen and temporal to things which are unseen and eternal. We have to do here in our present life with two worlds. Our communication with one, the world of matter, is by sense and science based on sense; our communication with the other, the world of spirit, is by faith and knowledge proceeding from faith. The two worlds, of course, are with God one system, and in this view there can be no contradiction ultimately between the truths of natural science and the truths of faith; between the economy of the life that now is, and the economy of the life to come. They must be at last, we know perfectly well, one economy. But they are not this at once for our present apprehension. On the contrary, they seem to be widely disparate orders of existence, that are in painful conflict on all sides, one with the other; so that it has been through all ages the great problem of life, how to harmonize their deep-toned discord. In the bosom of Christianity, especially, this conflict is brought to its fullest force and consciousness. It is the conflict here between nature and the supernatural, between science and faith, the history of which runs through all the Christian centuries; but the full crisis of which seems to have been reached only in our own time. Now it has become emphatically the burden of the world's universal life, the question of all questions for our universal modern civilization. It is moving the thunders of the Vatican in one way, and stirring the depths of all Protestantism in another way. It is taking hold of politics as well as religion; kings, princes, parliaments and statesmen are sorely troubled with its presence. All our science, all our business, all our education are entangled in the mighty dilemma one way or another, and have no power any more to hold themselves aloof from its practical challenge.

This it is, dear young friends, that forms, beyond all other considerations, the grand and solemn interest of the period in which you are called to live and work in the world, and that more than all else, to my own mind, throws an awful responsibility prospectively on your future lives. The critical struggle between the terrestrial and the supernal, to which I have now been directing your attention, is one in which you must all from this time forward, as children of your time and age, take more or less active part. You cannot be neutral in the warfare. It is too broad and deep for that. Not to be on the side of the Lord here, is to be on the side of Satan.

How faith and science are to be ultimately harmonized, I am not prepared to say. It is not necessary, it seems to me, that we should be able to solve the question in full in our present state. There are, however, four general propositions in the case, which we are bound to assert and maintain:

First. The conflict between the two spheres, as the world now stands, is not imaginary only, but most positively real, and it is growing in terrible significance every day. It has not been decided and ended yet, either on one side or on the other, and to ignore it is but the trick of the ostrich hiding her head in the sand to escape the hand of her pursuer.

Secondly. Science is not required to do blind homage to the authority of faith, exercised over it in an outward, mechanical way, according to the modern ultramontane theory of the Church of Rome.

Thirdly. Faith must not be required, on the other hand, to follow passively the authority of science, according to the fond view of the Spencers, Darwins, and

Huxleys of our day; the modern *Weltanschauung* in general, as it is called in Germany, by which naturalism and humanitarianism are made to take the place of the old supernatural faith altogether, and Christianity is found resolving itself into a new moral creation springing up from the earth, instead of a new spiritual creation in Christ Jesus, coming down from heaven.

Fourthly. Then we are bound, and for our faith also it is possible, to reverse this order of looking at the world, and so to organize our scheme of thought and life, that the earthly shall be felt with us to depend upon the heavenly, instead of the heavenly upon the earthly.

This does not mean any such wilful immolation of natural reason and conscience on the altar of religion, as the modern Jesuitic theory of Rome demands. But it does mean that the principle of the Christian faith, as supernatural, shall be regarded as independent of the principle of all mere natural life and science; and that in the relation of the two principles to each other, moreover, the first shall be held to be of higher authority always than the second, because in fact coming before this in the true *idea* of the world, however seeming to come after it in the actual world-process. In other words, the only true ultimate order both of essential being and of knowledge, in the general relation of the world of nature to the world of spirit, is in reality not from below upward, but from above downward—not a scaling of the heavens by the powers of the earth, but a flowing down upon the earth of the powers of heaven. That, therefore, is the only law of harmony in the end between nature and the supernatural, between the human and the divine (illustrated and enforced by universal analogy in the natural creation itself); and faith, as independent of science and greater than science, consists just in the power of seeing and owning this, whether it be able at the time or not able, to see in what way actually the claims of science are to be reconciled with its demands. If need be, faith can afford to wait for the final and full resolution of that "conflict of ages," till these outward heavens shall pass away as a scroll, and this panoramic time-vision shall lose itself at last in the light of the world that lies beyond time.

Need I say that the principle of Christian faith in this independent character, is not an abstract thought of any kind; the idea of the Absolute or Unconditioned in the sense of Kant or Sir William Hamilton, or that pure nescience which regards the infinite as the simply unknowable and unknown, in the sense of Herbert Spencer and the modern Humanitarian school generally? The principle plants itself, not on an abstraction, but on the very inmost reality of the world's actual being, which it is just the province and the special power of faith then (in distinction from sense, Heb. xi. 1–3) to authenticate and make sure to our human consciousness.

This objective reality is nothing other than the word of God, which is present as a living power in all divine revelation, as it has been spoken at sundry times and in divers manners through ages past by the prophets.

It is of His word in such wide general view God Himself speaks, Is. lv. 8–11, where He says: "My thoughts are not your thoughts, neither are your ways my ways. As the heavens are higher than the earth, so are my ways higher than your ways, and my thoughts than your thoughts. For as the rain cometh down, and the snow from heaven, and returneth not thither, but watereth the earth, and maketh it bring forth and bud, that it may give seed to the sower and bread to the eater; so shall my word be that goeth forth out of my mouth; it shall not return unto me void, but it shall accomplish that which I please, and it shall prosper in the thing whereto I sent it."

It is of the word in the same broad sense that St. Peter also speaks (1 Pet. i. 23–25), where he says of Christians that they are "born again, not of corruptible seed, but of incorruptible, by the word of God, which liveth and abideth for ever." To which he adds immediately: "All flesh is as grass, and all the glory of man as the flower of grass. The grass withereth, and the flower thereof falleth away; but the word of the Lord endureth forever. And this is the word which by the gospel is preached unto you."

But what the divine word is in such supernatural and really objective view comes ultimately to its full, absolute sense and force, as we know, only in our Lord and Saviour Jesus Christ, who is the Word Incarnate, the Divine Personal Logos, the eternal Son of God, incorporated into the very life of the world through union with our fallen nature, and made to be thus the Son of Man, for the great work of man's redemption. And here it is emphatically, therefore, that the grand descending order of God's creation comes fully and overwhelmingly into view, stultifying and turning into contempt the humanitarian imagination of an earth-born or earth-produced heaven in every shape and form.

"Ye are from beneath," we hear Him say; "I am from above: ye are of this world; I am not of this world. I said therefore that ye shall die in your sins; for if ye believe not that I am he, ye shall die in your sins" (John viii. 23, 24).

And so in our text: "No man hath ascended up to heaven but he that came down from heaven, even the Son of man which is in heaven."

This is the Christian *Weltanschauung*, in difference from every world scheme that starts from below, from the premises of mere nature, from the study of man as the highest out-birth simply of the world in its present state, and claims the right then of measuring the possibilities of the infinite and eternal by the rules of science drawn from the empirical and purely terrestrial sphere.

And who will dare to say that this stand-point of faith, found directly and immediately in the historical heaven-descended fact of Jesus Christ (the deepest truth of the world, if Christ Himself be true), is less rational or sure, either for the right understanding of life, or for the right use of life, than the posture of science undertaking to scan or scale the spiritual heights of creation from any lower position?

Say not, that this supernatural, heaven-descended fact is itself, since Christ has returned to heaven, no other now than a theological theory or doctrine. It is still before us as an ever-living fact in the evangelical history, and it lives also through the ages in the faith of the holy Catholic Church. We have it in the Apostles' Creed. That Creed depends in no way on science. It is at once and in its own right, the vision of what is highest, and therefore deepest also, in the constitution of the world's life, flowing down directly from God the Father through Christ, as the power of a new creation needed in this way to complete the sense of the old.

Here, then, is the great practical issue to which we are brought by our subject: the issue of ages, which, I have said before, is upon our own time, perhaps, as on no previous time, and the full solemnity of which you are now called to meet in passing out into the world. The conflict between unbelieving science and faith, between nature and the supernatural, between the powers of what St. Paul calls "this present evil world" and the "powers of the world to come;" in one word, between the spirit of anti-christ, denying that Christ is come in the flesh, and the spirit of true faith, confessing this great mystery of godliness; this conflict, I say, which underlies so profoundly the seething, tumultuating forces of the time, is one in which you also are now called to take active side and part, and which you have no power to escape.

Let me urge upon you then the importance of not throwing yourselves forth upon the open sea of life, in these circumstances, without the ballast of firmly established principle; without the compass of heaven-directed intelligence and thought; without the rudder of a resolute Christian purpose and will; only to be at the mercy of all winds and waves, and to float hither and thither with any current into which you may happen to fall. That would indeed be unworthy of your education, and might well cause us to feel that our labor bestowed upon you had been in vain. But I hope and trust better things of you, though I thus speak; and therefore it is that I call upon you on this occasion, to look the question before you squarely in the face, and to meet it at once in a full and clear-minded decision.

In the language of Joshua's farewell charge to the tribes of Israel, let me say to you now, in this parting address: "Choose ye this day whom ye will serve;" and let your right election, made now and here, stand as the solemn memorial of a covenant between you and God, to be remembered in all time to come. Before you are the two

Weltanschauungen, the two great world schemes, to which I have been directing your attention at the present time: the humanitarian theory of thought and life on the one hand, making spirit the outbirth of nature,—the celestial, the sublimation simply of the terrestrial; and on the other hand the theory of Christ and Christianity, and of the Apostles' Creed, resolving the highest life of the world in the down-flowing life of heaven. In the face of this alternative, let me ask, what think ye of Christ? Whose son is He? "Whom say ye," He asks of you Himself, "that I the Son of man am?" Here is the test at last of all true Christianity, whether doctrinal or practical. See that the right answer to it, as of old with Nathanael and Simon Peter, be with you also the one glorious guiding star of your lives.

"Do not err, my beloved brethren. Every good gift and every perfect gift is from above, and cometh down from the Father of lights, with whom is no variableness, neither shadow of turning. Of His own will begat He us with the word of truth, that we should be a kind of first-fruits of His creatures" (James i. 16–18). "Ye, therefore, beloved, seeing ye know these things before, beware lest ye also, being led away with the error of the wicked" (the naturalistic, humanitarian scoffers of the age), "fall from your own steadfastness. But grow in grace and in the knowledge of our Lord and Saviour Jesus Christ. To Him be glory both now and forever. Amen. (2 Pet. iii. 17, 18).

www.ingramcontent.com/pod-product-compliance
Lightning Source LLC
Chambersburg PA
CBHW020811230426
43666CB00007B/960